The Talk About *TransHERmation* Workbook Next Level Edition...

TransHERmation is a refreshing read that speaks encouragement to all women. It really doesn't matter who you are or where you are along your journey—we are all constantly transforming more and more into the image of Jesus. This book ministers truth to women about their identity in Christ. You will be challenged to develop yourself into being your personal best. The insights offered regarding the processes of deliverance and discipleship are authentic jewels that will build women, as they pursue their destiny in Christ. Lakeea is real, relatable, and relevant! You will be blessed through her transparency, practicality, and humor. *TransHERmation* is every woman's story! ~ **Patrice Burrell, Psalmist, Author, Certified Life Coach, Ocoee, FL**

Awesome book! Once you start reading it, it's hard to put it down because it sparks your interest to the point that you want to keep reading to see what's next. It can definitely help someone who has gone through some stuff...a must read! ~ **Cynthia Little, Certified Mentor and Coach, Nashville, TN**

Captivating book! You will not put it down. The transformation of Lakeea's life journey gives you insight on how to transform. ~ **Margaret Kirk, Prophetess and Marketplace Entrepreneur, Battle Creek, MI**

I have known Lakeea by *name* since high school. However, since reading *TransHERmation*, I feel as though I know her *personally*! After reading *TransHERmation*, I realized, Lakeea and I have similarities that I never knew existed, such as being a teenage mom, our educational goals, along with tackling similar trials and tribulations in life. However, throughout the book, Lakeea gave multiple Scripture verses that reminded the reader that through God, all things are possible! I then began to wonder if my past trials and tribulations *Transformed* me to the diligent medical professional that I am today!

The addition of a workbook to her book will be an asset to ANY WOMAN who needs to prepare for her *TransHERmation*! ~ **Sirmara Pierce, BSN, RN, CMC, LNC, Battle Creek, MI**

This will help any woman! The book is simply a must read! It's easy to read and follow, and it keeps your attention. I believe reading the testimony of Lakeea's transformation will inspire women to want it for themselves! Once that seed is planted, it will literally set a woman up to face the giants in her life...or the things that look like giants—things that only God transforming you can change. ~ **Sierra Stevens, Entrepreneur, Battle Creek, MI**

It has impacted my life and given me hope in that I am not who man says I am but who God called me to be. He will never leave me or forsake me. It also helped me through my weight-loss journey. I knew I did not want to leave 2018 the same way I came in. It has helped me elevate. It continues to help me; and because I have a good relationship with the author, I can see the fruit of what she means by *TransHERmation*. ~ **Robmieka Gibson, Administrative Assistant, Battle Creek, MI**

LAKEEA KELLY

Trans HER Mation

WORKBOOK

How God Can Take Everything You've Been Through and Transform You for His Glory!

"TransHERmation: How God Can Take Everything You've Been Through and Transform You for His Glory! Workbook" by Lakeea Kelly

Cover design, editing, book layout, and publishing services by KishKnows, Inc., Richton Park, Illinois, 708-252-DOIT

admin@kishknows.com, www.kishknows.com

ISBN 978-0-578-46944-7

All rights reserved. No part of this book may be reproduced, distributed, or transmitted in any form or by any means, including photocopying, recording, digital scanning, or other electronic or mechanical methods, without the prior written permission of the publisher, except in the case of brief quotations embodied in critical reviews, and certain other noncommercial uses permitted by copyright law. For permission requests, please contact Lakeea Kelly at lakeeakelly@gmail.com.

All Scripture references are taken from the **King James Version (KJV)** unless otherwise noted.

Some Scripture references may be paraphrased versions or illustrative references of the author.

Scriptures noted as **NLT** are taken from the **New Living Translation**, Copyright © 1996, 2004, 2015 by Tyndale House Foundation. Used by permission of Tyndale House Publishers, Inc., Carol Stream, Illinois 60188. All rights reserved.

Scriptures noted as **NKJV** are taken from the **New King James Version**®. Copyright © 1982 by Thomas Nelson. Used by permission. All rights reserved.

Scriptures noted as **NIV** are taken from THE HOLY BIBLE, **NEW INTERNATIONAL VERSION**®, NIV® Copyright © 1973, 1978, 1984, 2011 by Biblica, Inc.® Used by permission. All rights reserved worldwide.

Scriptures noted as **NASB** are taken from the **NEW AMERICAN STANDARD BIBLE**®,

Copyright © 1960, 1962, 1963, 1968, 1971, 1972, 1973, 1975, 1977, 1995 by The Lockman Foundation. Used by permission.

Scriptures noted as **ESV** are taken from The ESV® Bible (**The Holy Bible, English Standard Version**®). ESV® Text Edition: 2016. Copyright © 2001 by Crossway, a publishing ministry of Good News Publishers. All rights reserved.

Copyright © 2018 by Lakeea Kelly

Printed in the United States of America

Table of Contents

Chapter 1: Matters of the Heart 1
Chapter 2: A Made-Up Mind 13
Chapter 3: The Humility of Wisdom 23
Chapter 4: Attributes of a Woman of Meekness 31
Chapter 5: Relationships and Soul Ties 37
Chapter 6: Embrace Your Differences! 45
Chapter 7: Love Your Neighbor as Yourself 57
Chapter 8: Yes, Jesus Loves Me 63
Chapter 9: NO MORE DELAYS! 71
Chapter 10: Investing in Yourself 77
Chapter 11: Crowned Lady: Wearing Your Priestly Garments 81
Chapter 12: Words of Wisdom 89
Bonus Chapter: Fasting 91
Appendix A 97
Resources 99

Chapter 1

MATTERS OF THE HEART

A made-up mind

TransHERmation begins with a made-up mind. Did you know that the mind and the heart share the responsibility for your emotions and affections? When God created us, He created us with a heart, mind, and soul, and together, these make us a whole person. Our heart, mind, and soul are to be one with Jesus Christ, because He desires *all* of us. The mind, heart, and soul have the same functions; however, the *heart* is the center of them all. I will call the heart the one that "leads" the mind and soul. It is the heart that determines the paths that we take, the decisions that we make, and the emotions that we feel. What is in the heart affects our mind and enters our soul. The Bible tells us to guard our heart, because **"Out of it flows the issues of life." Proverbs 4:23 (KJV)** It is with our hearts that we "believe unto righteousness." The result of righteousness is a converted or changed heart. A heart that has its' affections, passions, emotions, thinking processes, and will set on the things of God is a converted heart that will produce good things. Salvation through Jesus Christ comes from a surrendered heart. As you can see...it all starts with the heart.

The heart can be overloaded and clouded with the things of the world, such as past hurts, rejection, bitterness and depression, strife, anger, unforgiveness, murder, sexual immorality, blasphemy, theft, false testimony and slander, and so much more. A heart that is full of these things can cause a delay in your process of moving forward in your destiny and purpose. It is very difficult to identify your purpose in life when you have a heart that has not been healed and delivered from rejection, depression, anger, strife, unforgiveness, jealous, envy, shame, doubt, perversion, etc. Woman of God, there is a seed inside you that is lying dormant waiting to produce—waiting to give birth to your destiny. Take a moment and read **Chapter 17** in my book *TransHERmation—"How God Can Take Everything You've Been Through and Transform You for His Glory!"* In this chapter, I talk about seeds.

Nurturing the seeds in our hearts

The seed that Jesus Christ plants in our hearts never dies while we are here on Earth. It does not matter if that seed was planted in you as a child, a teenager, or an adult. It doesn't matter if you grew up in the things of God and fell away, or if you believed in the gospel of Jesus Christ but did not fully surrender your heart. The seed of Jesus Christ is still inside you, waiting for you to fully surrender. It is waiting to be nurtured by prayer, worship, praise, the Word of God…and through your very words of life! While you are here on Earth, bring *life* to that seed.

Do you know that when God plants the seed of Jesus Christ in our hearts, He also *names* that seed? He may call your seed apostle, prophet, evangelist, pastor, teacher, author, business owner, educator, inventor…take a moment and read ***Jeremiah 1:4-5***. Just as God knew and called Jeremiah a prophet before he was formed in his mother's womb, He knew and called us as well. God is not a man that he should lie. He does not remove what He has called us, but he keeps the seed in our hearts while we are here on Earth until we respond. The only way that it will not be produced is if we die without responding. A seed can only grow if it is nurtured.

Excerpt from Chapter 17: *"Seeds can remain dormant for weeks or even years before they produce. I found out that there was a scientist by the name of William James Beal who started a 100-year-long experiment. He put seeds into 20 time capsules and dug one up every five years. The experiment is still going on today, and the researchers who are carrying on his work have found that some of the 25-year-old seeds can still sprout. It has also been noted by a scientist by the name of Jane Shen-Miller that the oldest living seed to germinate is over 1000 years old."*

How do I determine the issues that are in my heart?

In this chapter of the workbook, I am going to assist you with identifying "issues of the heart." Before you can begin to discern the will of God for your life, you must deal with the issues of your heart. A healthy and pure heart will bring light to the will of God for your life. I want you to take a moment to worship and pray before we begin this journey of TransHERmation. Play your favorite worship song or instrumental prophetic music softly in the background and say the prayer below. Do not limit your prayer to this *specific* prayer; but instead, allow the Holy Spirit to direct you. Trust what comes from your heart in this prayer. Remember, the heart is also a carrier of our emotions. If negative emotions arise as you pray, ask God to remove them and to show you the root of where they are coming from. It is important that you remain open and willing to accept what the issues of your heart are. There are times when we can be in denial (I have definitely been there) but trust that God knows you better than you know yourself. Remember…as they come up, *release them*. I am going to help you with this process. Before we begin, take a moment to read these Scriptures regarding the heart. I also want you to do the exercises below before you go into prayer to help you with determining the issues of your heart.

1.) Read **Matthew 15:17-20**: This Scripture clearly tells us that the words that come out of our mouths are what defile us and make us unclean. Think about the words that you use. Are they consistently negative or impure? Do you speak words of defeat? Do you gossip or lie? Is there unforgiveness or jealousy in your words? What about your thoughts? Are they evil, impure, or ungodly? The thoughts that are in your *mind* are reflective of what is in your *heart*. Are you operating in any of the ways that are listed in this Scripture? Based on this Scripture, write down those things in the space below pertaining to the questions asked.

My Words Are...	My Thoughts Are...

2.) What is your outer countenance or facial expression most of the time? Read the following Scriptures that talk about your outward appearance and facial expressions. Reflect on them and write down your thoughts as you read.

Proverbs 27:19:

_____
_____

Proverbs 15:13:

_____
_____

Proverbs 17:22:

_____
_____

Ecclesiastics 8:1:

_____
_____

Proverbs 16:15:

_____
_____

Isaiah 3:9:

_____
_____

Proverbs 25:23:

_____
_____

3.) What are those areas in your life that you place the most value on? What are the areas of your life that motivate your decisions? Are there any areas that you constantly think about? Are there areas in your life that are distracting you by keeping you away from devoting time to God or to your family, vision, and purpose? Read the Scripture below and note your answers in the space provided. I want you take some time to ponder on what you place value on and if any of those things are getting in the way with your relationship with God or are you moving forward in your God-given identity and purpose.

Matthew 6:21: "Wherever your treasure is, there the desires of your heart will also be." (NLT)

- **I place the most value on:** _____
- **I am motivated by:** _____
- **Areas my mind is constantly returning to:** _____
- **Distractions that keep me unfocused:** _____

Reflections on a humble heart

After reading and meditating on the Scriptures and answering the questions above, you should be at a place of reflection. Your heart should be soft and tender, ready for the Holy Spirit to begin His transforming work. Reflection of the heart often brings about humility because you can see the areas where you truly need God to heal and deliver. **Matthew 23:26** states, **"Blind Pharisee! First clean the inside of the cup and dish, and then the outside also will be clean."** The Pharisees were concerned about following traditions and rules in order to make themselves appear righteous, but they neglected the heart. "A pure heart will promote you into your God-ordained purpose and destiny." King David was promoted because of his heart, not his outward appearance. (There is so much more to the heart that I would love to share with you. I have a six-week e-course that is directly related to this workbook where I go deeper and expound more extensively on the topics covered in this workbook; but for now allow, the Holy Spirit to impart in you a new thing that is transformed into a woman of TransHERmation.) Go ahead and finish reading the Scriptures below and allow the Holy Spirit to minister to you as you get ready for worship and prayer. Make sure that you include the areas that you wrote about in the exercises above in your prayer. Ask God to deliver and heal! I am standing in agreement with you, Woman of God! I am excited about your journey!

- ***Proverbs 4:23: "Guard your heart above all else, for it determines the course of your life." (NLT)***

- *Luke 6:45: "A good person produces good things from the treasury of a good heart, and an evil person produces evil things from the treasury of an evil heart. What you say flows from what is in your heart." (NLT)*
- *Matthew 15:17-20: "Anything you eat passes through the stomach and then goes into the sewer. But the words you speak come from the heart-that's what defiles you. For from the heart come evil thoughts, murder, adultery, all sexual immorality, theft, lying, and slander. These are what defile you. Eating with unwashed hands will never defile you." (NLT)*
- *Romans 10:10: "For it is by believing in your heart that you are made right with God, and it is by openly declaring your faith that you are saved." (NLT)*
- *Matthew 15:8: "These people honor me with their lips, but their hearts are far from me." (NLT)*

Worship: Do not rush through your worship! Worship welcomes the presence of the Lord and the working power of the Holy Spirit. If you speak in a heavenly language, begin to speak. Speaking in your heavenly language builds your spiritual muscles and opens you up to receive divine revelations from God. Take this time to tell God who He is to you. Take this time to thank Him. You can even sing before Him during this time.

Worship Adoration:

*"Dear Heavenly Father, I worship you and adore you! You are an Awesome God! You are a wonder-working God, and I worship and praise you. Lord, You are so worthy, and there is none like You. Lord, I exalt you and praise your Holy Name. Lord, I thank you for your goodness and mercy. Lord, I thank You for being a God of compassion, mercy, and justice. I thank you for being the Mighty God; the Prince of Peace, the Wonderful Counselor, and my Great Deliverer. I worship You for being the **Alpha** and **Omega**... the **Beginning** and the **End**... the **First** and the **Last**. I worship you, O God, as the Door, the Gate, and the Truth to everlasting life. I worship you as the Bright and Morning Star, the Lion of Judah, and as the Great I AM! I worship you as the Shepherd of my soul. I thank you for your goodness and mercy and for your loving kindness. Lord, I thank you for supplying all of my needs according to your riches in Glory (continue to give God thanks and tell Him who He is to you).*

I come to you asking forgiveness for _____ (ask God to forgive you from everything that comes up in your spirit as well as those areas that you are already aware of). I repent for _____. Lord, I ask you to cleanse me, and purge me from all unrighteousness. Lord, I thank you for making my sins whiter than snow and refining me as silver and gold. Dear Heavenly Father, continue to reveal to me the areas in my heart and soul that are getting in the way of my relationship with you and preventing me from walking in my God-given purpose. Let your will be done in my life."

Allow the Holy Spirit to have His way with you and continue to pray as the Holy Spirit leads you.

Healing the broken pieces

Once the Holy Spirit has released you from prayer, begin to write down the broken areas of your heart that God revealed to you in the space below. Believe and trust God that those areas of your heart have been removed. Do not be discouraged if you do not see immediate results in every area, because there is a healing process that you must go through. In addition, there are some areas of the heart that have been there for so long that it takes a greater level of prayer and fasting for them to be uprooted. Do not be tempted to stop praying, but continue to pray and fast until you experience great breakthroughs in your life. This will be a continuous journey throughout your life. I highly recommend and encourage you to fast. (See bonus chapter in the back of this workbook on fasting.)

_____
_____
_____
_____
_____
_____
_____
_____
_____
_____
_____

As you go over what God revealed to you, begin to ask the Holy Spirit where and when each area first entered into your heart. In other words, what was the "point of entry"? Many times, it is something from our childhood, or possibly a toxic relationship in adulthood that opened the door for the issues of the heart, while other issues may have been passed down through generations.

I am teaching you to learn to partner with the Holy Spirit on your journey of TransHERmation. He is your Teacher, Comforter, Strength, and Advocate. You will learn how to be a friend of Jesus Christ on this journey.

Identify the point of entry for these areas below – depend on the Holy Spirit to reveal to you the root of the issue. For example, if it's rejection, ask the Holy Spirit to reveal to you where the rejection first began.

Issue	Point of Entry

Begin to ask God to remove the memory of the trauma and to give you a forgiving heart. The Holy Spirit has most likely already dealt with your unforgiveness in some areas, but they may come up again in this section of healing. Go ahead and allow the Holy Spirit to do His work in you and to remove all of the "residue" that would try to linger.

Prayer and seeking God for your full deliverance is something that you will continue to do. This is not a one-time thing, but you are now closer to your TransHERmation than before you began.

Identify your triggers

Now you are going to write down some things that trigger these areas that are in your heart. What are some things that trigger rejection, anger, gossip, strife, etc.? (Some of your triggers may be the company that you are keeping or your associations. We will deal with this in another chapter.) It is always helpful to know the reason behind a specific behavior, as this helps facilitate the healing process. When you are able to identify the triggers, you are able to better resist the devil, because now you can identify who your devil is. You can recognize his plots, ploys, and plans, and deal with them before they even start. When you are delivered from the issues of the heart, it is important to identify and know your triggers so that the issues that have been dispelled from your heart do not quickly take root again. Your healing is a process, and it is important for you to be able to identify the reasons why you are doing (or not doing) certain things as you are walking out your healing.

Write down the triggers of rejection, anger, pride, or whatever else you are facing in the space below:

Issue	Trigger

As I have already stated, it is important to have a forgiving heart toward those that have hurt you, used you, or persecuted you. Forgive, and your Heavenly Father will forgive you. I know you are probably saying "It is hard for me to forgive…you don't understand what they did to me!" Holding on to past offenses will slow your progress and stop you from moving forward into your God-given purpose. Unforgiveness breeds bitterness, anger, physical ailments, and depression. We need others to forgive us for our shortcomings; therefore, we have to be willing to take on the heart of forgiveness and mercy.

After you have read the Scriptures below on forgiveness, write down the names of those that you need to forgive. Decide to release them and move on; just forget about it! **Philippians 3:12-13: "I don't mean to say that I have already achieved these things or that I have already reached perfection. But I press on to possess that perfection for which Christ Jesus first possessed me. No,** *dear brothers and sisters, I have not achieved it, but I focus on this one thing: forgetting the past and looking forward to what lies ahead." (NLT)*

- *Romans 12:14: "Bless those who persecute you. Don't curse them; pray that God will bless them." (NLT)*
- *Matthew 6:14-15: "If you forgive those who sin against you, your Heavenly Father will forgive you. But if you refuse to forgive others, your Father will not forgive your sins." (NLT)*
- *Colossians 3:13: "Make allowance for each other's faults, and forgive anyone who offends you. Remember, the Lord forgave you, so you must forgive others." (NLT)*
- *Mark 11:25: "But when you are praying, first forgive anyone you are holding a grudge against, so that your Father in heaven will forgive your sins, too." (NLT)*
- *Matthew 18:21-22: "Then Peter came to him and asked, 'Lord, how often should I forgive someone who sins against me? Seven times?' Jesus answered, 'I tell you, not seven times, but seventy-seven times.'" (NLT)*

Name(s) of Person(s) that you need to forgive:

_____
_____
_____
_____
_____
_____

After you have written that person's name down, I want you to bless them by writing a prayer of blessing over their life. Re-read **Romans 12:14** above. The Word of God says to bless those that persecute you; and as you follow what the Word of God says, a great release will take place. It is important for us to follow the pattern of the Word of God.

Write a prayer below, blessing the person that you need to forgive. Continue to pray for the person until your heart feels good and not evil towards that person:

Chapter 2

A MADE-UP MIND

When I was battling depression, there were strategic steps that I took to overcome it. In this chapter, I will help you to utilize those same strategies.

Renew your mind

Now that you are on your way to having a healthy and pure heart, and now that you know what to do when you are facing issues of the heart, you can focus on a new mind. When issues of the heart are dealt with, you are now able to have a mind that thinks on things that are "good, lovely, praiseworthy, and of good report." You have emptied some of the negative things out of your heart, and now you need to fill your heart with His Word. Remember, all of this is a process, and you should consistently be applying **Chapter 1: "Matters of the Heart"** in your walk with Jesus. It is so important to read the Word of God daily. The Word of God is how you get to know who Jesus is and His character. It is through God's Word that you are cleansed and sanctified. The Word of God will help strengthen and comfort you in your time of weakness and will serve to encourage, rebuke, and correct you. The reading of the Word of God will be written on your heart, and the words and thoughts that are written on your heart will in turn affect your mind. **Proverbs 23:7: "For as he thinketh in his heart, so is he: Eat and drink, saith he to thee, but his heart is not with thee." (KJV)** From the Scripture above, we can see that the words on our hearts affect how we view ourselves. You can utter one thing out of your mouth, but what is your heart really saying?

I had a heart full of confusion, shame, guilt, and doubt, which caused an open entry for the enemy to plant lies in my mind, telling me that I was not forgiven by my Heavenly Father. I was tormented day and night with depression.

Take the time now to read **Chapter 8, pages 61-65** in *TransHERmation*, where I talk about my journey through depression, and then move over to **Chapter 15: "The Helmet of Salvation and the Holy Spirit."**

Excerpt from Chapter 15: *"Back in Apostle Paul's time, the helmet was put on as a protector for the head, face and back of neck. If there was a blow to the head, the rest of the armor would be of little use. One terrible blow to the head could cause brain injury. If brain injury occurs, you could lose your speech, become paralyzed and experience memory loss. The brain controls the rest of the body's functions. Several hits to the head can potentially be dangerous and can cause internal bleeding and wounds. You are of no use to fight in the battle if you have had an injury to your head: it would be too hard to fight, and it will make you vulnerable to a quicker death, so you would need to depend on your battle buddy to fight for you."*

Battle Buddies

In the space below, identify who your "battle buddies" are. Battle buddies are those people that you KNOW have your back and will stand in the gap for you through prayer when times get hard; when you want to give up, throw in the towel, and quit. Who can you call on that will have your back? Put down your pride and open up to someone that you can trust. As long as we are on this Earth, there will be trials and tribulations; and as sisters in Christ, we are to carry each other's burdens. **Galatians 6:2: "Carry each other's burdens, and in this way you will fulfill the law of Christ." (NIV)**

Look up *Ecclesiastes 4:9-10* and write it on the lines below. This is your "battle buddy Scripture."

_____
_____
_____
_____

TransHERmation

Before you begin to write down the names of your battle buddies, I want you to think of those relationships that you have that may be toxic. You may be wondering, "Why do I need to do that?" and "How does that line up with the next exercise?" The reason is because you may be considering having your battle buddy as someone that you are in a close relationship with that does not necessarily have a relationship with God. This may be the very person that has contributed to the issues of your heart. Ask yourself, "Is this a person that I am always tempted to gossip with? Is this a person that every time I am in their presence, I become angry and ready to fight?" Maybe this is a person that tempts you to get drunk, smoke weed, lie, or commit sexual sins? If you are depressed and feeling hopeless, discouraged, or to the point of wanting to give up, staying connected to the wrong person will not help your breakthrough, it will only keep you further in bondage. ***I Corinthians 15:33: "Do not be misled: bad company corrupts good character." (NIV)***

Write down the names of the individuals that will *not* be a good battle buddy, (i.e., an individual that will not effectively have your back.) This person is not capable of praying on your behalf, encouraging you through the Word of God, or providing you with sound wisdom. Your battle buddy will be honest with you and will NOT flatter you with lies. Check out the Scriptures below:

- ***Proverbs 27:5: "Better is open rebuke than hidden love." (NIV)***
- ***Proverbs 28:23: "Whoever rebukes a person will in the end gain favor rather than one who has a flattering tongue." (NIV)***
- ***Proverbs 24:25: "But to those who rebuke the wicked will be delight, And a good blessing will come upon them." (NIV)***
- ***Proverbs 27:6: "Faithful are the wounds of a friend, But deceitful are the kisses of an enemy." (NASB)***
- ***Proverbs 29:5: "A man who flatters his neighbor is spreading a net for his steps." (ESV)***

Toxic Relationships:

1. _____
2. _____
3. _____

4. _____
5. _____

Battle Buddies:

1. _____
2. _____
3. _____
4. _____
5. _____

*Side note: If you cannot think of anyone that you consider to be a battle buddy, then I highly recommend you revisit **Chapter 1**. Are there some rejection, abandonment, or trust issues going on that have prevented you from allowing God to bring genuine relationships into your life? Begin to pray that God will send you genuine friends. He will do it! I am a witness!

Until God brings those trusted individuals into your life, go to a pastor, counselor, teacher, or parent. It is important that you identify someone. Remember, kill the PRIDE!

Pray through the Psalms

Go to the **Psalms**, and identify some "go-to" chapters that you can read as prayers when you don't know exactly what to pray or when you are at a point where it's too hard to pray. If you don't even know where to begin (and we've all been there), pick up your Word, and start with **Psalms 31, 32, 34, 35, 54** and **63**. (And remember...we *do not* pray curses or wish ill-will on people. When we pray against our enemies, we are referring to the demonic spirits at work, and the devil.)

List your "go-to" chapters in the **Psalms**. Add to this list as you continue your journey of TransHERmation.

_____
_____
_____
_____

Look up the following Scriptures on the mind and write them in the space provided. Become familiar with these Scriptures and read them out loud for the next thirty days or until you become disciplined enough to cast down every vain imagination that exalts itself against the will of God for your life.

Philippians 4:8 _____
_____

2 Timothy 1:7 _____
_____

2 Corinthians 10:5 _____
_____

Colossians 3:2 _____
_____

I Corinthians 2:16 _____
_____

Isaiah 26:3 _____
_____

Philippians 4:7 _____
_____

Take control of your thoughts

The enemy will use your *thoughts* to affect your *emotions*, which in turn will delay your *progress*. For example, if I am having thoughts that tell me that I am worthless or that nobody wants me, those thoughts will affect my emotions and cause me to become depressed. Depression causes a stagnation in progression and leads to hopelessness, fear, torment, despair, pain, and sadness. Remember – *one seed can produce a lot of dysfunctional traits.* It's time to cast down those thoughts.

What are some thoughts that constantly plague your mind? Write them down in the space below. Remember this is a process and a journey. Although you have already dealt with the issues of the heart, the enemy will always try to come into your mind and plant lies. We must learn to combat his lies. Some of the lies he uses against us include...

- *"I am worthless"*
- *"I can't do this"*
- *"No one will want me"*
- *"I am ugly"*
- *"No one will support me"*

After you write down the lies of the enemy that plague your mind, combat those lies by writing down the opposite. For example, if it is "I can't do this," you will combat this lie by saying "I can do all things through Jesus Christ that gives me strength." If it is "I am ugly," you will write, "I am beautiful inside and out." This is a perfect time to spend some time in the Word identifying Scriptures that combat the lies of the enemy. If you need some Scriptures to help you get started, see the **Resources** section at the back of the book.

Thoughts That Plague Your Mind	**The Opposite of Those Thoughts**

In the space below, write down a prayer thanking God for revealing to you through His Word the opposite of those lies that the enemy has spoken to you (refer to the column – The Opposite of those Thoughts). This prayer should focus on thanking Jesus for showing you who you are in Him and rebuking who the devil says you are. This type of posture in prayer is very effective because you are approaching the throne of grace with confidence and boldness, knowing that He is perfecting everything that concerns you. In addition, it tells God that you are fully persuaded and have the faith that He is producing good fruit in you, including *love, kindness, goodness, self-control, joy, peace, faithfulness, and gentleness.* He is also producing *courage, boldness, hope,* and a *sound mind.* The posture of thanksgiving in prayer tells God that you trust Him, although it may not have fully manifested in the natural. You are speaking these things in the confidence that they have already come to pass. As it is written: **"I have made you a father of many nations. He is our father in the sight of God, in whom he believed-the God who gives life to the dead and calls into being things that were not." Romans 4:17 (NIV)** I have provided you with a sample prayer to help you as you are writing your own.

"Thank you, Jesus, that I have a sound mind. Thank you, Jesus, that I am filled with your peace, joy, love, and power. Lord, I thank you that I am bold, courageous, and filled with your Spirit. Thank you, Jesus, that I am walking in an abundant life on Earth. Thank you, Jesus, that I am the head and not the tail; above and not beneath. Thank you, Jesus, that I am favored by you. Lord, I thank You that I am fearfully and wonderfully made. Thank you, Jesus, that when you created me, you created me to be in your image. Thank you, Jesus, that you think good of me and not evil. Lord, I thank You that I have a hope, and an expected end in You. Lord I thank you that I am an overcomer and victorious through Jesus Christ. Thank you, Jesus, that I can do all things through Christ that gives me strength! Lord, I thank you that you became poor that I may become rich. Lord, I thank you that I am favored by you and your face is shining upon me. Thank you, Jesus, for leading me by the hand and directing me into all truth. Thank you, Jesus, for your wisdom, knowledge, and revelation. Lord, I thank you for prospering me in every area of my life. Thank you for your healing, deliverance, and complete restoration to my original purpose and position in you. In Jesus' Name, Amen!"

_____
_____
_____
_____
_____
_____
_____
_____
_____
_____
_____
_____
_____
_____

Get up and get out!

As I dealt with depression, I had to force myself to "get up and get out." I forced myself to put on my makeup. I went to the mall. I went to go get a massage.

In the space below, write down some things that you enjoy doing. Is it painting your nails? Is it going to the movies? Is it a quiet evening alone with a nice meal?

Some of you have been caught up in your current circumstances and life's trials and tribulations. You are so busy making sure that everyone else is okay that you've neglected to take time out for yourself. Because of this, you may not even be sure what you like anymore. Maybe you are the kind of person who feels guilty if you take time out for yourself. This is the time to throw all of that out the window, and think about transforming yourself so that you can be a whole person...a healthy woman of God, inside and out, for yourself and for others.

After you have written down the things that you enjoy doing, set a date and time this week to make it happen. Everything doesn't cost money. You may enjoy taking walks and you haven't done so because you are "down in the dumps" or depressed. Make up your mind today that you will do what you enjoy! NO EXCUSES!

Things I Enjoy Doing...	Date Completed

Chapter 3

THE HUMILITY OF WISDOM

Heavenly wisdom or demonic deception?

As God is cleansing you from things that are in your heart and mind, it is important for you to continue to fill those places with the counsel of the Lord. It is very important for you to follow His instructions, which are laid out in the Word of God. The Book of Proverbs is an instruction manual on wisdom. It provides us with wise counsel and advice on life. **Proverbs 9:10: "The fear of the LORD is the beginning of wisdom, and knowledge of the Holy One is understanding." (NLT)** In order to obtain wisdom from God, you MUST fear Him. To fear Him means to be in awe and reverence of Him and to delight in Him and in His Word. A heart and mind that delights in God and His Word produces much wisdom; but in order to know wisdom, you must have a genuine interest in God and His Word. You cannot pretend to have an interest in God and call it wisdom… that would be hypocrisy. Before we look at the Book of **Proverbs**, turn to **James 3:13-18**. We are going to look at the difference between heavenly wisdom and demonic deception.

Write **James 3:13** in the space provided and underline the following words: "meekness" or "humility of wisdom" (depending on the translation that you are using). I have written out the New King James Version for you – try using another version so that you can compare the two.

"Who is wise and understanding among you? Let him show by good conduct that his works are done in the meekness of wisdom." (NKJV)

_____
_____
_____
_____

- **Meekness:** Meekness is to be humble and gentle, and fully submissive to God without reacting out of anger, fear, or rejection. TransHERmation truly begins when the spirit of meekness is rooted in your heart. Pray for a meek heart daily!
- **Wisdom:** Divine wisdom that comes from God – ideas of infinite skill, insight, knowledge, and purity.

Reread **James 3:13**, considering the Hebrew-Greek definition of meekness and wisdom, and write in your own words in the space below how it speaks to you.

_____
_____
_____
_____
_____

My example: *"A wise person is one that demonstrates good conduct and good deeds or works out of a heart of humility – gentleness and purity; with total submission to God."*

Write **James 3:14** in the space below, and underline the following words: "bitter envy" and "self-seeking." (Some Bible translations say "bitter jealousy," "selfish ambition," or "strife.")

_____
_____
_____
_____

Whose agenda are you promoting?

Think about the words "bitter envy" and "self-seeking or strife." An individual that harbors bitter envy or is self-seeking is an individual that only thinks of themselves. They are looking to promote their own agenda. They have wrong motives and are seekers of pleasure, riches, and fame, and boast only in themselves. The strife in their hearts is due to the war in their members (body) for the pleasures of this world. They seek to possess what belongs to someone else, which leads to envy, and envy in turn produces strife. Self-seeking or selfish ambition also produces covetousness, i.e., a strong desire for material possessions or a strong desire to have that which belongs to another individual. **James Chapter 4** will explain this more. **James 3:15: "This wisdom does not descend from above, but is earthly sensual, demonic." (NKJV)** If this is going on in your heart, return back to **Chapter 1**, and deal with the matters of the heart. Remember...the matters of the heart are ongoing, not a one-time thing. If there is jealousy, bitterness, envy, selfishness, or covetousness in your heart, do NOT sin against the truth by boasting of your wisdom. Your "wisdom" is sensual – carnal, earthly, and full of lust for the things of this world.

Write **James 3:16** in the space below, and underline the following words: "confusion" and "evil."

_____
_____
_____
_____

Confusion: uncertainty, disorder, unstable. You do not know you are a Kingdom citizen (uncertainty of residence). You do not identify with the Kingdom dictates but instead rely on worldly wisdom.

Evil: Spoken of evil deeds.

If you are operating out of envy and selfish ambition, you are considered "out of order." You are unstable and full of uncertainties. But most of all, you are uncertain of your residence (Selah). Pause and ponder on that for a minute. TransHERmation cannot take place in your life when you are uncertain of who you are, who you belong to, or your citizenship. In order to be a citizen of the Kingdom of God, you must live by the Kingdom dictates, rules, and laws. Our dictates come from the Holy Bible. **Ephesians 2:19: "Consequently, you are no longer foreigners and strangers, but fellow citizens with God's people and also members of his household." (NIV)**

Write **James 3:17** in the space below, and underline the following words: "pure," "gentle," "mercy," "without partiality," "without hypocrisy," or "without sincerity."

_____
_____
_____
_____
_____

Pure: Holy of God; perfect.

Gentle: Mild mannered; courteous; appropriate; polite; respectful.

Mercy: To show compassion.

Without partiality: not open to distinction or doubt; unambiguous – clear-cut.

Without Hypocrisy: Sincere; not pretending.

James 3:18: "Now the fruit of righteousness is sown in peace by those who make peace." (NKJV)

Examine your motives

Take a moment to think about something that you have been praying for. Is there anything that you have been praying and asking God for out of a heart of jealousy, envy, or covetousness? Have you been desiring worldly pleasures, or someone else's possessions, gifts, or talents? You need to be very honest and ask God to search your heart. Write down the things that you are believing God for in the space below, and then pray and ask God if your heart is pure towards everything you are asking Him to do in your life. Is what you are asking for out of selfish ambition, so that *you* can boast and get the glory, or so that

God can get the glory? Be very honest. You are being transformed. As you write those areas down, take notes as to anything that the Holy Spirit reveals to you. Repent, and ask forgiveness when necessary.

James 4:3 "You ask and do not receive because you ask amiss, that you may spend it on your pleasures."

_____
_____
_____
_____
_____
_____
_____

The dangers of the "if onlys"

There are times when you can undermine who God has destined you to be because you are comparing yourself to the next person. You may be looking at how skilled they are or what they have, and saying, *"If only I had her voice." "If only I could pray like her." "If only I had her money." "If only I dressed like her."* The list goes on and on. You may have even mimicked the behaviors or looks of someone else because you are not comfortable with who you are or were operating out of jealousy or covetousness. This is not of God or wise as we see in the Scriptures we just read. God created you in His image and He wants to leave a mark and a legacy on the Earth *that can only come through you*. Be encouraged, and take this time to read **Chapter 23**.

Excerpt from Chapter 23: *You are created for His purpose, and you add value. It is not in your title that you add value or your degrees, profession, job title, marital status, economic status, the house or car you drive, but because you are "You" – you add value. So many people begin to identify themselves with the things that I just named; and if one of those things is taken away, they feel they have lost value. Do you know your smile, hug, presence, and conversation add value? I believe God wants us to know who we are before He gives us the promise. He checks our heart's motives before He gives us status in the Kingdom or even status on Earth. He does not want us to identify with the* *gift more than the gift-giver. He wants us to be able to function in whatever situation we are in. He wants us to trust that when He created us, He created a masterpiece.*

"Wisdom then is not what I know, wisdom is how I live. And so how I live according to the wisdom of God is a barometer on my spiritual condition." ~ John McArthur

The consequences of lacking wisdom

Let's take some time and look at the Book of **Proverbs**. Read a chapter in the Book of **Proverbs** daily and write down the key points regarding wisdom and other wise counsel that Solomon provides in each chapter. See **Appendix A** at the back of this book for a worksheet to help you as you journal through this exercise.

Reflect on the lessons that you have learned, and the consequences of lacking wisdom. This is a time for you to reflect on what you could have done differently in life based on the chapters that you have read, or the lessons that you have already learned. For example, there was a time in my life when I was always hasty in my decisions and only prayed *after* the consequences came, which was so unwise. I learned from Scripture to not make hasty decisions but to pray and seek God first. **Proverbs 19:2** taught me this: **"Desire without knowledge is not good-how much more will hasty feet miss the way!"** I had to learn not to jump out and do things without having a full understanding or knowledge first and reminding myself that it may sound good, but is it really what God wants for me?

As you work through the Book of **Proverbs**, take the time to note special lessons that jump out at you here. Record the date, and keep this journal as a way to thank Him as you pray. If you need more space, see **Appendix A**.

Date	Lesson/Reflection

God said that all we have to do is pray for wisdom and He would give it to us freely. ***James 1:5: "If you need wisdom, ask our generous God, and He will give it to you. He will not rebuke you for asking."***

Chapter 4

ATTRIBUTES OF A WOMAN OF MEEKNESS

Being meek can often be viewed as being weak, fearful, or timid. Some have even equated it with being a "doormat." Meekness has been portrayed as a woman in the movie "Coming to America" with Eddie Murphy. Whenever Eddie Murphy asked his potential wife a question, she would say, *"Whatever you like."* Whatever he asked her to do, she was totally submissive to him, to the point of her hopping on one foot and barking like a dog. This is not what Jesus calls being meek in regards to coming under agreement with something that is clearly wrong in God's eyes and according to the Word of God. It is all in our response – showing humility in the face of adversity. But on the other hand, we *should* have the "whatever you like" attitude when it comes to fully submitting ourselves to Jesus Christ. Think and ponder on that for a moment! Do you have a "whatever you like" response towards your relationship with Jesus Christ?

Meekness is a calling

A woman that is meek is actually very powerful and wise (as we read in **Chapter 3**), strong and valued in God's eyes. She is someone that is not easily angered or given over to strife. The meek woman is able to exercise self-control, while knowing who she is in Jesus Christ. She doesn't have to prove a point by saying things that are ungodly, rolling her neck or eyes, or even "saying things" without actually saying a word, e.g. a haughty look. I have been there ladies, but God is requiring us to master the spirit of meekness. If you are rude, unkind, and disrespectful because "it's your personality," or by saying things like "This is just how I am," you are operating in a level of pride and will need to pray to the Father for the spirit of meekness. Don't get me wrong, being meek is not a "woman only" characteristic; a meek and gentle spirit is part of the fruit of the spirit. But, since we are talking about TransHERmation, I will be addressing women.

Being meek is not about being a quiet woman that sits in the corner with her head hung low. Being meek is about knowing when to respond and when to be quiet. (Side note: not everything requires a response. Meekness is not agreeing with something that is contrary to the Word of God but is having the wisdom to know how to respond in the face of adversity or falsehood.) I know I'm repeating myself, but *some things are worth repeating so that they can resonate in our spirit*. Learn to ignore criticism and move forward as if it doesn't exist. If you do not master the art of ignoring it, you will constantly be distracted by what people say and how they feel. Your focus will not be on the things of God, and the purpose and destiny that He has for you. Mastering the art of ignoring the criticism keeps you moving forward in your purpose. There will always be criticism. Not everyone will like you, be for your ministry, or follow Jesus Christ.

We will take this time to look at examples in the Bible of how Jesus walked in the spirit of meekness. Read the following Scriptures.

- **Matthew 11:29: "Take My yoke upon you and learn from Me, for I am gentle and lowly in heart, and you will find rest for your souls."**
- **I Peter 2:23: "...who, when He was reviled, did not revile in return; when He suffered, He did not threaten, but committed Himself to Him who judges righteously."**
- **Isaiah 53:7: "He was oppressed and He was afflicted,
  Yet He opened not His mouth;
  He was led as a lamb to the slaughter,
  And as a sheep before its shearers is silent,
  So He opened not His mouth." (NKJV)**
- **Hebrews 4:15: "For we do not have a High Priest who cannot sympathize with our weaknesses, but was in all points tempted as we are, yet without sin." (NKJV)**
- **2 Corinthians 10:1:" Now I, Paul, myself am pleading with you by the meekness and gentleness of Christ—who in presence am lowly among you, but being absent am bold toward you." (NKJV)**

TransHERmation

Look up the following Scriptures below and in the left column write down the characteristics that do not display meekness; and on the right, characteristics that display meekness. For example, easily angered; prideful; unkind; teachable; slow to speak, and quick to listen, kind, etc.

Scripture	No Meekness	Meekness
Leviticus 19:18		
Psalm 141:3		
Proverbs 10:12		
Proverbs 14:29		
Proverbs 15:1		
Proverbs 15:7		
Proverbs 15:18		
Proverbs 16:32		
Proverbs 18:21		
Proverbs 19:11		
Proverbs 20:22		
Proverbs 21:23		
Proverbs 24:29		
Proverbs 29:11		
Proverbs 29:20		
Proverbs 29:22		
Proverbs 31:30		
Isaiah 5:21		
Matthew 5:7		
Luke 17: 3-4		
Romans 12: 17-21		
Ephesians 4: 26-27		
Ephesians 4: 32		
James 1:9		
James 1: 26		

Proverbs 14:1: "A wise woman builds her home, but a foolish woman tears it down with her own hands."

Cultivating a meek and humble spirit

A woman of wisdom is a peacemaker in her home. She builds up, blesses, and encourages with her tongue and does not tear down her home by walking in dissension or strife.

Proverbs 16:24: "Kind words are like honey—sweet to the soul and healthy for the body." (NLT) WOW...kind words can even bring forth healing to the body.

Take this time to honestly answer the questions below. If you answer yes or respond negatively to most of the questions, begin to ask God for forgiveness and repent. Ask Him to fill your heart with a meek and humble spirit. Please do not go into condemnation if you are not currently operating out of a spirit of meekness. Jesus loves you, and it is His will for us to be free.

1. *How do you respond when someone disagrees with you?*

2. Are you easily irritated and offended?

3. *How do you handle stress?*

4. Are you quick to hold grudges or are you quick to forgive?

5. *Do you feel like you must always have the last word to prove a point?*

6. Are you argumentative and critical?

7. *Do you lack self-control when it comes to your mouth or in your response to someone else's actions?*

8. Do you find yourself impatient with others and always finding fault?

9. *Do you retaliate against those that have done you wrong, or do you trust God to vindicate you?*

10. Where are some areas that you can demonstrate more meekness, e.g., at work, school, on the job, ministry, your enemies, etc.? Write down specific examples.

The Bible tells us to pursue peace.

Psalm 34:14: "Turn away from evil and do good. Search for peace, and work to maintain it." (NLT)

Hebrews 12:14: "Work at living in peace with everyone, and work at living a holy life, for those who are not holy will not see the Lord." (NLT)

To live at peace with your enemies does not mean that those people will become your best friends, but it *does* mean that you will not repay evil for evil. You will not be in strife with them or speak ill-spoken words. You will bless and not curse.

The danger in your words

Did you know that slanderous, abusive, ill-spoken words make you a murderer at heart? Or that anyone who hates a brother or sister is a murderer at heart? (See **Proverbs 18:21 and I John 3:15**.) It doesn't take an actual gun to kill someone…you can kill someone with your tongue, and that is not the heart of God! *REPENT AND REFUSE TO BE A MURDERER!*

Let us take the time to look at **Matthew 5:21-26**.

"You have heard that it was said to those of old, 'You shall not murder, and whoever murders will be in danger of the judgment.' ^{22} But I say to you that whoever is angry with his brother without a cause shall be in danger of the judgment. And whoever says to his brother, 'Raca!' shall be in danger of the council. But whoever says, 'You fool!' shall be in danger of hell fire. ^{23} Therefore if you bring your gift to the altar, and there remember that your brother has something against you, ^{24} leave your gift there before the altar, and go your way. First be reconciled to your brother, and then come and offer your gift. ^{25} Agree with your adversary quickly, while you are on the way with him, lest your adversary deliver you to the judge, the judge hand you over to the officer, and you be thrown into prison. ^{26} Assuredly, I say to you, you will by no means get out of there till you have paid the last penny." (NKJV)

Read the whole passage, and then write down on the lines below what God places on your heart regarding these specific verses.

Verse 22: This verse is another example of speaking slanderous, abusive words over your brother or sister. Depending on your translation, the two words that stand out in this verse are "Raca" and "fool." Raca means "to speak slanderous abusive words towards someone," and a fool is someone who is "dull, empty, or godless." This type of behavior comes from someone that purposely wishes ill will or death over someone.

_____
_____
_____
_____
_____

Verse 24: In this verse, pay attention to the words "gift" and "reconciled." Gift: "to give." Used in the context of gifts given as an expression of honor to God. Your gift at the altar may be your prayers, worship and praise, spiritual gift(s), or giving of your monetary resources.

Reconciled: "To have peace, change your feelings towards." We cannot offer our gifts before God with offense or unforgiveness in our hearts and expect Him to accept our gift or honor our prayers. The effectual prayers of the righteous avail much. Therefore, we must have a repentant heart when we come before God. If you do not quickly change your mind regarding the thoughts of your brother or sister – i.e., fellowman (Christian or friend, neighbor, any other person irrespective of nation or religion with whom we live or whom we chance to meet), God will not accept your gift.

Chapter 1: Matters of the Heart is so important; and it is the first chapter of this workbook for a reason. We must consistently ask God to search us and cleanse our hearts from all unrighteousness so that we can be in right relationship with Jesus Christ. Forgive and reconcile quickly!

Chapter 5

RELATIONSHIPS AND SOUL TIES

*Disclaimer: this chapter is **not** for women that are facing marital issues or concerns. This chapter is **not** to give advice regarding marriages. Please seek God, use wisdom, and follow godly counsel as it pertains to your marriage.*

Examining your relationships

When you are moving forward into your God-given purpose and assignment, it is so important to have the right, godly relationships in your life. The wrong relationships can sabotage your destiny and your relationship with God. At this point in your life, when you are ready to be transformed into what God has called you to be, you must ask yourself, "Is my relationship with God and walking out my destiny in God more important than pleasing man?" There are times when we do not want to leave toxic environments or people because we have a lack of self-worth. We are concerned about what people may think. We may also be afraid to end the relationship because there is a "soul tie." A negative soul tie is when there is a linkage of two souls that brings forth negative results and manifestations. Turn to **Chapter 18: Relationships and Ungodly Soul Ties**.

Excerpt from Chapter 18: *"Demonic and negative soul ties will cause you to operate in rebellion; you will begin to do things for the sake of that person or persons. Emotional soul ties will blind you to not think about the consequences of your actions. The person begins to be your idol because you have now set your affections on nothing but that individual. The Word of God says for us to put no other gods before Him. When we put all of our affections onto an ungodly relationship, it is idolatry."*

Negative, ungodly soul ties can cause you to operate in a way that is contrary to your identity. You may begin to wonder what it is that you truly have a passion for, because you took on someone else's passions and identity. You may find yourself acting in a way that is out of character for you. For example, when a person is under the influence of alcohol, their perceptions and responses are distorted, and they do things that are out of character. This is what happens when someone is connected to toxic, ungodly relationships. You begin to take on the characteristics and attributes of another person.

Excerpt from Chapter 18: *"When a person has lost their identity, they lose the capacity to make the right decisions. They are influenced by the demonic and the ungodly soul ties. Even their appearance becomes distorted, meaning they will wear clothes or hairstyles that they normally would not wear, their words and language become corrupted, their emotions are unstable, and the demonic spirits (that were already present) are magnified."*

Watch your mouth!

Look up the following Scriptures and write in the space:

- ***Ephesians 4:29: "Don't use foul or abusive language. Let everything you say be good and helpful, so that your words will be an encouragement to those who hear them." (NLT)*** (Some translations say "corrupt communication" or "unwholesome talk.")

Write some examples of foul, corrupt, unwholesome, or abusive language that you have used in the past or currently use. Examine those words and ask yourself if those words are helpful or encouraging.

_____
_____
_____
_____
_____
_____

I Corinthians 15:33: "Do not be misled. Bad company corrupts good character." (NIV)

_____
_____
_____
_____
_____
_____
_____

Toxic people – toxic relationships

Are you in companionship or fellowship with someone (or a group of people) that is toxic? If so, are you participating in those toxic behaviors? Have you ever found yourself demonstrating good habits, but once you started hanging around evil company, your good habits were broken?

Take this time to examine your closest relationships. How do those relationships benefit you? How do they build you up and strengthen you?

- Are they encouraging and pushing you to be your best?
- Are they an asset or a liability?
- Are you the only one giving (time, prayers, resources, encouragement, money, support, or just friendship in general), while they are taking – taking – taking?

List each of your closest relationships below, and answer the questions above pertaining to each one. (If you need more space, there is additional space in the **Appendix** at the back of the book.) Depending on how you answered the questions, it may very well be time for you to cut away and let go of those toxic relationships so that you can grow and be all that God has called you to be. Toxic relationships are detrimental to your walking out the purpose and destiny for your life. Once you connect to the right relationships, you will flourish, grow, and multiply.

Name	Relationship	Benefit

Look up the following Scripture and write in the space:

1. ***2 Corinthians 6:14: "Do not be yoked together with unbelievers. For what do righteousness and wickedness have in common? Or what fellowship can light have with darkness?"***

_____
_____
_____
_____
_____

Yoke: "To be in companionship or partnership with unbelievers. Another of, a different kind; two different natures. Participate in what they do."

Yoke: "To yoke unequally, that is, to yoke two different kinds of animals together to pull a load."

Look at ***Deuteronomy 22:10: "Thou shall not plow with an ox and a donkey yoked together."***

Scenario: Imagine two different animals that are yoked together, trying to pull a load. A bird and a lion, or a dog and a pig. Two different animals with two different natures. Consider the Scripture above regarding an ox and a donkey.

The nature of the beast

List some of the different natures of the donkey and ox. For example, the donkey is much faster than the ox; the ox is much stronger than the donkey. If you are not able to identify with the different nature of the ox and donkey, think of two different animals that you are familiar with and list some differences.

Now think of it in terms of yourself. Being yoked together with someone that has a different nature than you. How far do you think you would get? Imagine having a business partnership with someone that has a different nature than you. You want to operate with integrity, but they want to manipulate and deceive. You value customer service but they are rude. Those are just a couple of examples.

In addition, look in terms of the Fruits of the Spirit – **Galatians 5:22-23**. ***"But the fruit of the Spirit is love, joy, peace, longsuffering, kindness, goodness, faithfulness, gentleness, self-control. Against such there is no law." (NKJV)***

List some other examples below of how a relationship will look that has two different natures.

_____
_____
_____
_____
_____

According to the Word of God, a good-natured individual that is in fellowship with an evil-natured individual will always be corrupted or influenced by the bad nature. Meditate and read the Scriptures below pertaining to this comment.

Write the following Scriptures below:

- ***I Corinthians 6:16:***

    _____
    _____
    _____
    _____

- ***I Corinthians 15:33:*** _____
_____
_____
_____

Read the following passage: **Haggai 2:10-14**

"On the twenty-fourth day of the ninth month, in the second year of Darius, the word of the Lord came by Haggai the prophet, saying, 'Thus says the Lord of hosts: 'Now, ask the priests concerning the law, saying, 'If one carries holy meat in the fold of his garment, and with the edge he touches bread or stew, wine or oil, or any food, will it become holy?'

Then the priests answered and said, 'No.'

And Haggai said, 'If one who is unclean because of a dead body touches any of these, will it be unclean?'

So the priests answered and said, 'It shall be unclean.'

Then Haggai answered and said, 'So is this people, and so is this nation before Me,' says the Lord, 'and so is every work of their hands; and what they offer there is unclean.'" (NKJV)

The fruit that you bear

Words of counsel to the single ladies: If your desire is to have a God-fearing man in your life, make sure that *you* are bearing good fruit. We all have areas in our lives that need improvement, but make sure that your life exemplifies the nature of a godly woman. Make sure you are practicing righteousness. We all make mistakes...but if your "mistakes" are *habits* then it's a lifestyle! Keep pursuing God and seeking Him to perfect those areas that lack fruit. Refer to **Galatians 5:22-23**. In addition, make sure the man that you are interested in – or that is interested in you – is bearing fruit and practicing righteousness. Your gauge should be the fruit.

My husband and I were friends for approximately four years before we began a relationship, and his nature never changed. He was consistent. I cherished the friendship that I had with my husband before we actually entered into a relationship because of the fruit he bore – he was consistent as a man of God. He didn't start showing me a different kind of lifestyle or character after we were married…his fruit remained during friendship, courtship, and marriage. Ladies, *pay attention to the fruit* during friendship and courtship.

Is there fruit that follows his works? For example, he may go to church, fast, tithe, read the Scriptures, operate in the gifts of the spirit, and pray regularly… *but what type of character is being produced out of those works?* Because someone can do all those things and have NO CHARACTER!

Jesus' Example

Your relationship with unbelievers, or those of a different nature than you, should always be one of "purpose." For example, Jesus ate with sinners to disciple, teach, heal, and deliver. His relationship with the unbeliever was *always on purpose*. It was to disciple and teach the path of righteousness that leads to eternal life with Him. We as believers have a mandate to teach and preach the gospel of Jesus Christ and to draw people closer to Him. Is your life with unbelievers "on purpose?" All believers should have a purpose to disciple, witness, teach, heal, and deliver unbelievers. *Part of your Christian walk is to disciple unbelievers and lead them to a relationship with Jesus Christ.*

For the Believer

Read the following passage: ***I Corinthians 5:9-11***

"When I wrote to you before, I told you not to associate with people who indulge in sexual sin. But I wasn't talking about unbelievers who indulge in sexual sin, or are greedy, or cheat people, or worship idols. You would have to leave this world to avoid people like that. I meant that you are not to associate with anyone who claims to be a believer yet indulges in sexual sin, or is greedy, or worships idols, or is abusive, or is a drunkard, or cheats people. Don't even eat with such people" (NLT)

- Why do you think Paul instructed believers not to keep company with someone that calls himself a brother or sister but indulges in sexual sin, is greedy, worships idols, is abusive, drinks too much, or cheats people? (Vs. 11)

_____
_____
_____
_____
_____

Remember, our job is to restore our sister or brother out of a spirit of gentleness and love. If your brother or sister refuses to repent, do not keep company with them; but continue to pray and fast for them, that they will be restored back to the faith of Jesus Christ.

Read **I Corinthians 6:9-10** and **Galatians 5:20-21**, and underline who will *not* inherit the Kingdom of God.

"Don't you realize that those who do wrong will not inherit the Kingdom of God? Don't fool yourselves. Those who indulge in sexual sin, or who worship idols, or commit adultery, or are male prostitutes, or practice homosexuality, or are thieves, or greedy people, or drunkards, or are abusive, or cheat people—none of these will inherit the Kingdom of God." (NLT)

"... idolatry, sorcery, hostility, quarreling, jealousy, outbursts of anger, selfish ambition, dissension, division, envy, drunkenness, wild parties, and other sins like these. Let me tell you again, as I have before, that anyone living that sort of life will not inherit the Kingdom of God." (NLT)

Take this time to read the prayer on **page 148** of *TransHERmation*.

Chapter 6

EMBRACE YOUR DIFFERENCES!

Cleaning your house

There may be times when you resist or neglect the uniqueness of who God has called you to be because you fear what others may think. Maybe you have been rejected in the past (or maybe you are being rejected now) and so you hide in your shell and do not allow God to use you for His purpose. I suffered from rejection for a long time; it started during my childhood. I will be honest with you...I wanted to be free from rejection so badly that I consistently sought out deliverance in this area; but the rejection was still there, lurking at my front door –the door to my heart. I had a "heart condition" of rejection that needed to be changed. My *mindset* had to be changed. I had to begin to see myself as *God* saw me, and I had to be okay with who God created me to be. It didn't matter that I was going through deliverance lines for rejection...do not get me wrong. I *believe* in deliverance, and I am *for* deliverance; my book talks about deliverance...however, there were some hidden deceptions in my heart and mind that had to change before I could experience true freedom. Someone may be asking, "Since you had the spirit of rejection cast out of you, doesn't that take care of the rejection?" That is an absolute NO! It is like cleaning up your house and getting rid of all of the garbage, or better yet, getting rid of all of the old clothes. For that moment, your house is clean, but you have to maintain your house in order to keep it clean. And when you get rid of those old clothes, you cannot welcome them back in! Garbage may enter, but you have to get rid of it when it comes.

The same thing is true of rejection. It still knocks at my door and tries to show up; but since I recognize who is at the door, I do not let it in. There have been times that I opened the door, but then I told rejection, *"You are not welcome because my house is clean, and garbage is not welcome here!"* and slammed the door! If by chance rejection makes its way into my mind or heart, I immediately get rid of it because I am too familiar with what it *looks* like, *sounds* like, and *feels* like. I refuse to go back, and Sister, you too need to refuse to go back to those people, places and things that God has delivered you from!

I had constant thoughts of: "I am not good enough." "What if I am not accepted?" "What are others going to think of me if I mess up?" **Excerpt from Chapter 14:** *If you are drawing back from walking in the fullness of who God called you to be because of someone else's opinion of you, know that their opinion is based on their own insecurities and issues.* Or maybe they have not had the opportunity to engage with someone that is different from "their world," and seeing you is uncomfortable because it is not "normal" for them. In addition to being concerned with how others viewed me, I also feared making mistakes. I didn't want to look bad in front of people; I wanted to bring my "A game" all the time.

The spirit of perfectionism

Pause for a minute: Some of you hesitate to "step out." You fear making mistakes because you have a "spirit of perfectionism." Perfectionism is not of God! I had to come to understand this and learn that making mistakes while walking out our God-given assignments brings forth growth. We will make mistakes, and a perfectionist does not take constructive criticism or correction well, because correction is perceived as "You have a problem with me." or "I must not be good enough." when that is not the case at all.

Maybe that isn't the case for you. Maybe you feel like Moses, who had a speech problem and didn't feel confident enough for God to use him to lead the people. **Exodus 4:10: "But Moses pleaded with the Lord, 'O Lord, I'm not very good with words. I never have been, and I'm not now, even though you have spoken to me. I get tongue-tied, and my words get tangled.'" (NLT).** God then told Moses, *"Isn't it I that created your mouth?"* God is saying that to you too! *"Isn't it I that created you for my purpose?"* Is rejection stopping you from embracing who God called you to be? Take this time to read **Chapter 14** in *TransHERmation*.

Excerpt from Chapter 14: *I didn't think I was good enough and often compared myself to others that appeared to be doing better than me. I was insecure in my own abilities and in who God created me to be. I judged the uniqueness of who God created me to be based on what someone else thought. I was willing to hide my true self behind a mask in order to pacify others and to feel accepted. Woman of God, you are uniquely made – His very own masterpiece. He is the creator of creation and therefore, He is expressed differently through every one of us. He does not express Himself in the same way. He made you who you are for His purpose, and He wants to express the creativity of His glory through you.*

Honoring the One who created you

You are fearfully and wonderfully made. God was in awe of you when He created you, and Jeremiah tells us that He *honored* what He created. Did you know that you are dishonoring God when you fail to embrace who He has called you to be? Let's look at the example of Moses again. Moses had a speech problem, yet God's reply was **"Who makes a person's mouth? Who decides whether people speak or do not speak, hear or do not hear, see or do not see? Is it not I, the Lord?"** God already knew your imperfections when He created you, and it is *through* those imperfections that His Glory is revealed in you.

Think about some areas in your own life where you feel there are some imperfections. This could be your skills and abilities, or maybe you have a physical limitation. For example, I have felt like Moses. At times I do not pronounce all of my words correctly, and sometimes get tongue-tied and nervous when I have to speak in front of a crowd. Write down your insecurities in the space below.

_____
_____
_____
_____
_____
_____

Look up and write out the following Scriptures. Identify the imperfection, weakness, or how others viewed them in each instance.

- ***Exodus 4:10-11***

- ***2 Corinthians 11:6***

- ***Acts 4:13***

- ***Jeremiah 1:6-7***

- ***Genesis 17:17***

- ***2 Timothy 1:7***

Did God not use these individuals because of their weaknesses? God is the Creator, and since He used these individuals...Woman of God, *He can use you too*!

Are there areas from your past or mistakes that you have made that you feel like God is holding against you? If so, list those areas below. Then go back, and next to every area, write *"I am forgiven."* Say it out loud, *"Jesus forgives me for _____."* Now thank Him for healing you from those areas that you have been holding on to!

_____
_____
_____
_____
_____
_____
_____
_____

Looking beyond our weaknesses

Now we are going to look at individuals that God used in the Bible that made mistakes or had a past, but yet God used them. Read the following Bible passages and write your thoughts.

1. Saul before he became Apostle Paul: **Acts 8:1-3;** The Conversion of Saul: **Acts 9:1-31; I Corinthians 15:9**

_____
_____
_____
_____
_____

2. Apostle Peter: **Luke 22:34, 54-62; Matthew 26:74; Matthew 16:18**

_____
_____
_____

3. Moses: **Exodus 2:11-15**

4. Gideon: **Judges 6:1-32**

Finally, let's look at some famous people who failed, but kept going until they succeeded. Google their stories:

- **Walt Disney** was fired from the Kansas City Star because his editor felt he "lacked imagination and had no good ideas."
- **Oprah Winfrey** was publicly fired from her first television job as an anchor in Baltimore for getting "too emotionally invested in her stories."
- **R. H. Macy** (Macy's Department Stores) had a series of failed retail ventures throughout his early career.
- **Katy Perry** dropped out of high school after her freshman year.
- Not a single record label would sign **Jay-Z** before he started his own.
- **Stephen's King's** first novel was rejected 30 times before it was published. Today, King has written over 50 novels that have collectively sold over 350 million copies.
- **Henry Ford** had two failures that resulted in bankruptcies.

There are many famous people that failed before they made it. We don't always know about those failures, because we see where they are now...but what if they had given up? *You cannot give up or allow failure and rejection to hinder where you are going.*

Rebuke the spirit of comparison

We have looked at both Biblical and natural examples of people that succeeded despite their weaknesses, past lives and mistakes, or because of being rejected by others. Woman of God, I have taken away all of your excuses for not moving forward in who God has called you to be. Do not allow rejection to stop you. There will be people that do not like you or do not understand your relationship with Jesus Christ. You will be rejected for righteousness' sake. (Read **Chapter 21** in *TransHermation: Being Called to Rejection: A New Perspective.)* Jesus was rejected by many during His time on Earth. Many did not believe that He was the Son of God. Although Jesus was rejected by many, He did not compromise His message or His assignment. Jesus did not allow the noise of the crowd to distract Him from His assignment; He knew who He *was* and who He still *is*! Amen!

Since you have no more excuses, write down your passions, talents, and things that you love to do below. What is it that you always had a passion for but because of rejection, you no longer do it? Maybe there is something that you have always enjoyed; painting your nails, doing your makeup, cooking, painting pictures, or writing songs.

_____
_____
_____
_____
_____
_____
_____

In the space below, write down some things that you like about yourself. It is almost always easier for us to identify with what is wrong with us than to name the things that we like about ourselves. We use these as excuses for why we cannot move forward in what God has called us to do. As we saw above, Moses tried to use his speech problem as an excuse, and Jeremiah tried to use being too young.

_____
_____
_____
_____
_____
_____

Now think about the things that you do not like about yourself. Is there something that you do not like about yourself that is keeping you from walking out what God has called you to do? Think about the areas where you have struggled with recognizing your own gifts and talents. Have you compared your singing, writing, speaking style, etc. to that of someone else, and so you have not allowed God to multiply your talents and use you, because you are focused on someone else? Determine that you will *not allow comparison to STOP you!*

_____
_____
_____
_____
_____
_____

Maybe you have not been comparing your gifts and talents with those of someone else, but you lack the boldness to step out. Another strategy that helped me overcome fear and timidity is staying connected to those that are bold and confident in who God called them to be. There was an impartation that took place in my life.

Excerpt from Chapter 20: *If you are experiencing the spirit of rejection, it should be cast out, but that is not enough. It is important to maintain your deliverance. I was able to maintain my deliverance by staying connected to individuals that did not have a spirit of rejection, people that walked in boldness* *and courage, and individuals who were comfortable in who they are and in being themselves. Seeing those types of people operate in the things of God with favor, prosperity and success was an impartation to my life.*

Begin to think about those you know that you can connect with who do not deal with rejection. An impartation will come into your life. If you do not know of anyone, pray for those genuine connections. Ask Him for role models, mentors, or a life coach.

_____
_____
_____
_____
_____

I am...

Take this time to seek the heart of God concerning you. Make sure you are not distracted. Silence your phone, turn off the television, and go to a quiet place where it is just you and the Lord. Begin to seek God through prayer. If you are holding any grudges, offenses, or unforgiveness in your heart, let those things go, ask for forgiveness, and repent. When we come before God in prayer, we want to make sure we forgive so that our Heavenly Father will forgive us and listen to our prayers. Begin to talk to your Heavenly Father. Ask Him who He says you are. Ask Him to describe you and begin to write what you hear below:

- I AM **FAITHFUL**
- I AM **BOLD**
- I AM **FEARLESS**
- I AM **BEAUTIFUL**
- I AM **KIND**
- I AM **SINCERE**
- I AM **LOVING**
- I AM **DISCERNING**
- I AM **FREE**

- I AM **LOVED**
- I AM **HUMBLE**
- I AM **GRACIOUS**

Who God says you are will be your declarations over your life. When you truly understand and *know* that God validates you, you will no longer rely on the validations of others. I became free when I accepted and embraced that God *chose* me, *loves* me, *validates* me, and *thinks well of* me. I came to understand that it is *okay* if I make mistakes in the process. As a child of God, I am open to the guidance and correction of my Father when I make mistakes. I trust that He will point them out to me and teach me along the way. *My mistakes do not discredit my calling or position in the Kingdom.* Please remember that! Will I pronounce a word wrong or get tongue-tied from time to time? Absolutely! But that does *not* disqualify me as a preacher or teacher for Jesus Christ. Maybe you miss a note while you are singing. Does that disqualify you from being a singer? Of course not! There is not a person alive that has not made mistakes. Someone who criticizes others for making a mistake or does not give grace where it is due, is operating in pride. In other words, they think they've got it all together and have no need for growth or correction (or a Savior for that matter!)

Stepping out

Begin to embrace what makes you different. What sets you apart from the rest? Most people do not step out because of rejection. There is a lack of faith in who God created them to be, and they are looking to themselves rather than looking at the One that created them. Put your trust in God. When you use what He has already given you, He will multiply your talents and open you up to more of who you are.

Take this time to read **The Parable of the Talents: Matthew 25:14-30**

"Again, the Kingdom of Heaven can be illustrated by the story of a man going on a long trip. He called together his servants and entrusted his money to them while he was gone. He gave five bags of silver to one, two bags of silver to another, and one bag of silver to the last—dividing it in proportion to their abilities. He then left on his trip.

The servant who received the five bags of silver began to invest the money and earned five more. The servant with two bags of silver also went to work and earned two more. But the servant who received the one bag of silver dug a hole in the ground and hid the master's money.

After a long time, their master returned from his trip and called them to give an account of how they had used his money. The servant to whom he had entrusted the five bags of silver came forward with five more and said, 'Master, you gave me five bags of silver to invest, and I have earned five more.'

The master was full of praise. 'Well done, my good and faithful servant. You have been faithful in handling this small amount, so now I will give you many more responsibilities. Let's celebrate together!

The servant who had received the two bags of silver came forward and said, 'Master, you gave me two bags of silver to invest, and I have earned two more.'

The master said, 'Well done, my good and faithful servant. You have been faithful in handling this small amount, so now I will give you many more responsibilities. Let's celebrate together!'

Then the servant with the one bag of silver came and said, 'Master, I knew you were a harsh man, harvesting crops you didn't plant and gathering crops you didn't cultivate. I was afraid I would lose your money, so I hid it in the earth. Look, here is your money back.'

But the master replied, 'You wicked and lazy servant! If you knew I harvested crops I didn't plant and gathered crops I didn't cultivate, why didn't you deposit my money in the bank? At least I could have gotten some interest on it.'

Then he ordered, 'Take the money from this servant, and give it to the one with the ten bags of silver. To those who use well what they are given, even more will be given, and they will have an abundance. But from those who do nothing, even what little they have will be taken away. Now throw this useless

servant into outer darkness, where there will be weeping and gnashing of teeth.'" (NLT)

What is it that you have been feeling in your heart that you need to step out and do? What is it that God has been telling you to do but you've resisted, because you have allowed fear to creep in? Maybe you know you are called to be a speaker, but you have been turning down God-given opportunities to speak. Do you have a talent for doing hair but are too afraid to take the steps to open up your own hair salon? Or do you love to write but are afraid to write a book, because you don't think anyone will want to read it? Maybe you want to be a lawyer but you're afraid to enroll in classes because you have been out of school for so long. You have people that are waiting for you! Get to work!

Courage is stepping out and doing the very thing that you are afraid of! Allow the power of God to ignite your faith!

Take this time to write down the steps that you are going to take that will move you closer to being who God has called you to be. And if there is something that you enjoy doing but stopped doing because of the fear of rejection, do that thing!

_____
_____
_____
_____
_____
_____
_____
_____
_____
_____

Chapter 7

LOVE YOUR NEIGHBOR AS YOURSELF

Mark 12:31: "The second is this: Love your neighbor as yourself. There is no commandment greater than these." (NLT)

Authentically prosperous

Woman of God! Woman of Wisdom! Woman of TransHERmation! You must first love *yourself* so that you can properly love, help, and support *others*. God is love, and in the beginning of this workbook, I directed you back to the heart of God because it starts with Him first. As a matter of fact, the first commandment is this: **Mark 12:30: "Love the Lord your God with all your heart and with all your soul and with all your mind and with all your strength." (NIV)** You can have a "dressed up" outside...and a corrupt and messed up inside. There are plenty of people who are successful on the outside (from the world's viewpoint) but are full of evil. There is no substance to who they are. Any success or prosperity that they have is superficial, because they are not solidified by Jesus Christ. A woman that is first changed from the inside has a renewed mind, seeks the heart of God and wants to please Him, and is marked as authentic and truly prosperous. I would rather have *God* pleased with me and solidify me, than to have the applause and praise of *people*. When you are "authentically prosperous" (I just made up a phrase and love it...LOL! Authentically prosperous...), there are earthly rewards and opportunities that God will bring to your life, and there is an eternal reward in Heaven with Him! Look up the following Scriptures regarding pleasing men, and write them on the lines below.

Galatians 1:10:

_____
_____
_____
_____

Ephesians 6:6:

_____
_____
_____
_____

John 12:43:

_____
_____
_____
_____

Luke 16:15:

_____
_____
_____
_____

After reading the Scriptures above, I hope you are moved to receive your reward, promotion, and applause from God! May you hear Him say, "Well done, Daughter!" If you are compelled to please others over first obeying and pleasing God, then you may be having an identity crisis, and an identity issue going on. There are some insecurities, such as low self-esteem and low confidence that are blocking your ability to see yourself through the eyes of Jesus Christ. In **Chapter 6**, I asked you to write down some of your insecurities. Go back and review them. Because of some of those insecurities, you are tempted to "dumb yourself down" and compromise your authentic self.

Excerpt from Chapter 14: *I didn't think I was good enough and often compared myself to others that appeared to be doing better than me, which is insecurity. I was insecure in my own abilities and in who God created me to be. I judged the uniqueness of who God created me to be, based on what someone else thought. For example, I loved to laugh and joke around; and if there was a bitter-serious person that would give me the look...you know the look, like, "All that laughing is not called for," it would cause me to draw back and keep a guard over how much laughter or how much of myself I would demonstrate around that person. I would adjust and hide the uniqueness of who God created me to be around those that misunderstood me; those that were too uptight, or too bitter. I judged my value based on their interaction or even their non-verbal reaction towards me. I didn't want to be disliked or an outcast. I was willing to hide my true self behind a mask in order to pacify others and to feel accepted.*

Authentically you

Part of my "authentic self" is one that loves to laugh, and as you can read from my excerpt from my book *TransHERmation*, you could see that I too faced insecurity. I want you to really think about your authentic self. I want you to ponder on the characteristics that make you "you." Also, think about those areas that you believe are misunderstood; but actually, it's your authentic "you." It's who God wired you to be. The authentic "you" is who God wants to use for HIS GLORY! As you are thinking and pondering on this section of the workbook, if what comes to you is *"I am rude, because I don't take no mess from no one, and my response comes off mean,"* know that is not what God desires for you! His desire is for you to be a kind, patient woman who responds well to others. We went over this in **Chapter 4: Attributes of a Woman of Meekness**. Hopefully, that is not your response, or you will have to go back in prayer and ask God to remove your toxic attitude, and God may reveal to you that you are bold. Your *authentic* self may be one that is bold, hates injustice, and protects those that cannot defend themselves. Your *authentic* self may be one that is quiet and does not have a lot to say; therefore, you are an introvert rather than an extrovert.

In the space below, write down your authentic self through God's eyes or those areas that you may feel are most misunderstood by others. Please note: Some of your characteristics and ways will directly line up with your purpose, calling, and gifting. That is another book by itself.

_____
_____
_____
_____
_____
_____

After you have written your authentic God-given self above, begin to reflect on what parts of you that you have compromised. This is a reflection moment! Write down those areas below and begin to ask God for RESTORATION!! Ask God to restore you back to your *authentic* self...the one that He created before the foundation of the world.

_____
_____
_____
_____
_____
_____

Let's take a look back at **Mark 12:31**: *"The second is this: Love your neighbor as yourself. There is no commandment greater than these." (NLT)*

Ask yourself...

1. Have I ever hurt someone or "done someone wrong"? If the answer is yes, did I ask for their forgiveness? Did I ask for God's forgiveness?

2. *Have I ever held a grudge against anyone? Has anyone ever held a grudge against me? How did I feel?*

3. Have I ever been unloving to someone? Has someone ever been unloving to me? How did I feel?

4. *Have I desired compassion and mercy from someone but they didn't give it? How did I feel?*

5. Have I ever experienced someone talking about me in a negative way? Have I ever talked about someone in a negative way?

The Golden Rule

I am sure you answered "yes" and experienced some hurt, unforgiveness, and letdowns in your lifetime from others, just as you have hurt, not forgiven, and let down others. To love your neighbor as yourself is to show the same forgiveness, kindness, patience, respect, and attitude towards someone that you would like to receive. It's called the **Golden Rule**, and it is found in ***Matthew 7:12: "Do to others whatever you would like them to do to you. This is the essence of all that is taught in the law and the prophets." (NLT)***

Love your neighbor as you love yourself, so that God can freely forgive you as you forgive others!

Chapter 8

YES, JESUS LOVES ME

In the previous chapter, we talked about rejection. The rejection that we experience can sometimes carry over into our relationship with Jesus Christ. I will speak personally regarding my own relationship with Jesus Christ before He freed me. I had the idea that God would be angry with me if I didn't measure up to what I considered my "standard," which was a standard of perfection. I am not referring to what God calls perfection (we will get into more of that shortly). I was fighting my desire to please both *God* and *people*. I didn't want God mad at me, and I didn't want people mad at me. Sometimes, my desire to please people outweighed my desire to please God. I was sometimes willing to compromise my true identity and who God called me to be, to please others.

Legalism or grace?

When I wholeheartedly decided to give my life totally over to God, I began to develop a strong desire to please Him, (which is not a bad thing to do) but my strong desire to please Him became legalistic in nature. I was serving God out of duty and obligation rather than a loving relationship between a Father and daughter. The definition of legalistic is *"adhering excessively to law or formula; especially to the letter rather than the spirit."* Legalism is in opposition with grace. Grace promotes inward change and renewal, while legalism promotes performance and an outward expression of righteousness without a changed heart. Legalism says that salvation is gained through good works, when in fact, we are saved through the work that Jesus Christ already did on the cross by shedding His blood. Through His blood, we have free access to Him, and through His blood, He cleanses us from all unrighteousness. It's a gift that we must *accept and receive...*not something that we work for. The good works that we produce should come from a changed heart and a renewed mind through Jesus Christ; not because we are somehow trying to gain His approval through works. This is where I was at. I felt like He only loved me if I followed strict guidelines without the working of the Holy Spirit in my life.

Book Excerpt from Chapter 14: *My fears of abandonment and rejection started to carry over into my relationship with Jesus. I was afraid that He would be angry with me when I messed up. I had this idea that He was a hard father that would be upset with me if I made mistakes. The wrong mindset and concept of God will tell you that He is mad at you and will not accept you unless you work your way to heaven—it dismisses the friendship and relationship with Jesus Christ.*

The wrong mindset will tell you that, "if I do not jump up and down three times, turn around, slap my neighbor, pray five hours a day, and fast with only water, then I am not saved or in relationship with Jesus Christ."

I am exaggerating, but you get the picture. I have been there—not to that extreme—but definitely in bondage to the idea of working my way to heaven without a true, loving relationship with my Heavenly Father, to the point where condemnation would set in because I did not feel I was worthy to be called His daughter.

Please read Chapter 14 before you continue.

A loving father

Jesus wanted me to view Him as a loving Daddy and not a dictating Father. He wanted me to trust that He thinks good of me, not evil. And even in His discipline towards me, He still loves me and thinks well of me. I am a mother of two young men, and there is nothing that would stop me from loving them—even in their mistakes. I will encourage, correct, and rebuke them because they are my sons. This is how our Heavenly Father is with His children. **Hebrews 12:6: "For the Lord disciplines those He loves, and He punishes each one He accepts as His child."** At one time, my relationship with Christ was in the posture of Him always disciplining me. I was always "in trouble," or so I thought.

There were times when I was busy doing "ministry" while neglecting my personal relationship with Jesus Christ. I thought that the more I did meant that somehow, God would be more pleased with me. I felt as if I had to earn His love, and it was hard for me to accept that He *chose me*, *died for me*, and *loves me unconditionally*. Declare over your life right now: Jesus *chose me*, *died for me,* and *loves me unconditionally* according to **I Corinthians 13:4-8**.

I felt every time I made a mistake or sinned unintentionally that He was angry with me and discounted me as His own. I didn't understand the power of the blood of Jesus. I didn't understand that Jesus shed His blood so that I could continue to come to Him for forgiveness, as long as I have a sincere heart. I remember a prophet prophesying to me that I needed to accept the blood of Jesus. The fact is, I suffered from rejection, and I felt as though Jesus Christ had rejected me too…but *that was far from the truth.* My idea of acceptance from Jesus Christ was obtaining salvation through works. **Ephesians 2:8: God saved you by His grace when you believed. And you can't take credit for this; it is a gift from God." (NLT)** Some people will avoid coming to Jesus Christ because they feel as if they somehow must prove they are worthy, not realizing that He accepts us where we are, and He does the "cleaning up." We do not have the power or ability to get ourselves "right." What Jesus Christ desires is an open, sincere heart that will say "Yes" to His grace, love, sincere counsel, and discipline. When we mess up, He expects us to get up and return to Him for cleansing and guidance. He is a loving Father that desires us to come to Him. Yes, He will discipline us, because a loving Father disciplines His child to bring forth righteousness.

Book Excerpt from Chapter 14: *Yes, Daddy disciplines his daughter because He loves her. He does not turn His back on His daughter because she makes mistakes or messes up from to time to time.*

Jesus loves you…flaws and all

Some people give up because they are trying to live a "never messed up," flawless life and feel like God is not worth serving because "who can measure up?" I had the "I need to measure up!" mentality. There were some moments where I was living up to man's standards and not God's. What man considered "holy" was not "holy" at all. Serving Christ out of obligation and not love is *not* holiness. Serving God out of a heart of obligation without love is unfruitful, and the peace and joy of God will often be missing from your life. I often felt like God was judging me based on my performance. Did I pray long enough? Did I serve enough? Was He going to answer my prayers if I slipped up on my fast? I remember receiving a prophetic word from the Lord. This lady said to me, *"Jesus loves you…and your flaws too."* I was left totally confused – how can God love my flaws? What she was saying was, "God loves me right where I am, and He isn't throwing me away because of my imperfections. He wants to refine me as silver and gold and create a precious diamond out of me." He desires to create a precious diamond out of you too. Boy, does Jesus love us. Don't run away from Him, but instead run to Him. He is the only one that can change your sinful nature into a righteous and holy nature.

"The Bible is filled with imperfect people who were used by God to accomplish His purposes." So, does God expect us to be flawless – make no mistakes, never fall short, never sin? The answer is *no*! If this were the case, there would have been no need for the blood of Christ, and no reason to have continuous access to Him. Once we totally surrender to Him, we are expected to live a righteous lifestyle and bear fruit, but at no time is it possible for us to **never** fall short in our walk with Him. We will be complete and perfected once these mortal bodies turn into immortal bodies. If you were expected to be perfect, you would never have the need to be corrected – such a person is full of pride.

What is God saying when He expects me and you to be perfect?

- **Be a person of integrity**: A significant part of integrity is humbling yourself before God and admitting your faults and sins. Confessing your sins before Him, repenting, and seeking forgiveness.
- **Be faithful**: Faithful does not mean flawless.
- **Obedience**: To do God's will without idolatry, serving no other god but Him.

Despite setbacks, remain faithful; despite mistakes, remain faithful; despite falling down, get back up and remain loyal.

TransHERmation

Read and study the lives of the individuals below. What mistakes did they make but yet God chose them?

Individual	Mistakes
Noah	
Jonah	
King David	
Peter	
Jacob	

Receive God's mercy and grace over your life. Read the following Scriptures:

Proverbs 28:13
I John 1:9-2:1
Psalm 86:15-16
Psalm 103:8-11
James 3:2
I John 1:8
I John 3:6-8
Galatians 6:7-9
Proverbs 24:16
Psalm 37:23-24
Lamentations 3:22-25

Temptations

We all have weaknesses and things that draw us toward temptation. Are there any weaknesses or temptations that you have, and do you find yourself being drawn to them? If so, list them below. Once you list them, ask yourself: Do I run to these situations or individuals, or do I avoid them? When you feel the temptation to fall into the trap of your weakness, do you approach the throne of grace by asking God for help through prayer? Ask God to help you not to yield to those temptations but to deliver you from evil.

Read the following Scriptures regarding temptation, and write them on the lines below:

Luke 22:40: _____

Matthew 6:13: _____

I Corinthians 10:13: _____

2 Timothy 2:22: _____

James 1:12-14: _____

James 4:7: _____

TransHERmation

I Peter 1:6-7: _____
_____
_____

Hebrews 4:15-16: _____
_____
_____

God allows temptations in our lives, but *He will never tempt us with anything that is evil*. We are tested with afflictions and trials to grow us and our character and to test our faithfulness towards Him. For example, God allowed Job to be tempted by the devil to test his obedience and faithfulness towards God.

Read the passage on Mary and Martha in **Luke 10:38-42**.

"As Jesus and the disciples continued on their way to Jerusalem, they came to a certain village where a woman named Martha welcomed him into her home. Her sister, Mary, sat at the Lord's feet, listening to what he taught. But Martha was distracted by the big dinner she was preparing. She came to Jesus and said, 'Lord, doesn't it seem unfair to you that my sister just sits here while I do all the work? Tell her to come and help me.'

But the Lord said to her, 'My dear Martha, you are worried and upset over all these details! There is only one thing worth being concerned about. Mary has discovered it, and it will not be taken away from her.'" (NLT)

Note some differences between Mary and Martha.

Mary	Martha

Let's look at **Vs. 42**; *"...but few things are needed—or indeed only one. Mary has chosen what is better, and it will not be taken away from her." (NIV)*

Choosing what is better

Is your life overloaded with too many things that have taken away your ability to hear God and receive from Him? Remember: *more* is not necessarily *better*!

Begin to write down everything that you do and are involved in. Now, compare how much time you spend on these things with how much quality time you spend with Jesus.

What are some areas that you can declutter from your life that will remove the heavy burdens and distractions? You may also need to consider decluttering your physical closet of some of those old shoes and clothes that you have had since "God knows when." Begin decluttering!

_____

_____

_____

_____

_____

_____

_____

_____

Jesus loves you…and it is not measured by how much you do or affected by what mistakes you make. He desires a heart of faithfulness, integrity, and commitment to His will!

Before you go to the next chapter: Read **Chapter 11** in *TransHERmation.*

Chapter 9

NO MORE DELAYS!

At this point, you should be ready to start pursuing your God-given purpose, and stepping into your gifts and talents, if you haven't started already. I truly believe that we have more than one gift, talent, and purpose; however, some of those gifts and talents do not begin to flourish until we start with what is already in front of us. These may be gifts and talents that we already know about, or maybe there is an assignment that God has already shown you, but you are not operating there at this moment.

Lay the foundation

Do not try to build the house without first laying the foundation. A house without a foundation will not stand. In other words, do not begin an assignment that God has shown you without first preparing for it. Preparation comes from building the foundation first. Let me provide an example of what I mean. Let's say God spoke into your spirit and told you that you are an entrepreneur and will own your own boutique and become a millionaire (Hallelujah, Amen!) You are operating in a lot of the characteristics and traits of an entrepreneur; however, you haven't counted the cost of the building. You haven't started saving or budgeting your money, you haven't determined the location of the building... you have done no preparation. Or maybe God has told you that you would be operating in full time ministry. You don't pray, read your Word, minister to the lost, give to the poor, etc....but you are ready to quit your job and start your ministry without any preparation. Are you believing in miracles but haven't exercised your faith? (I feel a preach coming on, so let me reel myself back in.) Take this time to look up **Luke 14:28-30** and write it on the lines below:

_____

_____

_____

_____

Preparation involves groundwork, planning, and training. Have you gotten any training, done the groundwork, or started planning? If the answer is no, then you are not ready to receive the full manifestation of the promise. God will reveal His destiny and plan for us on the Earth through the Holy Spirit; and once we say "Yes" and come under agreement with what He spoke to us, He will begin to prepare us. It is all in God's timing when the full manifestation comes forth—how long we are on the journey is up to God and our willingness to submit to the process of preparation.

The beauty of small beginnings

The process of preparation will stretch you and cause you to leave your comfort zone. It may cause pain, heartache, and tears, and will have ups and downs as well as gains and losses…but it is ALL worth it in the end. You will have a lot of "wins" during the process too. As you may have heard, *"Do not despise small beginnings."* The small beginning is the preparation for the major win. During our preparation, there are several stages of our assignments that God takes us through. My first assignment that God birthed out of me was as an intercessor. We are all called to pray, but He placed a *mandate and anointing* on my life to pray. Next, He birthed the preacher, and then my book *TransHERmation*. I am embracing the rest of my journey as I reach my ultimate goal in Christ Jesus. God developed me during the different stages of my life, and He trained me in different situations. Some of my training was through church, some through my jobs, some through relationships, and the tests that come with serving Him. At the very moment that you are reading this workbook, God has you on a journey of preparation, and I pray that you will embrace it to the fullest. Truth be told, a lot of our preparation started in our childhood. God was preparing me to preach at nine years old!

Excerpt from book: *It was at this age, nine years old, that I began to preach many sermons at home in front of the mirror. My mom never knew that I did this, but I would be preaching away. I recall making a sermon out of the song*

"Man in the Mirror" by Michael Jackson. I wish I could go back and listen to some of those sermons that I preached. When someone asks me how long I have been preaching, my answer is, "Since I was nine years old!" I didn't have an audience...and I didn't need one.

I never thought that what I was pretending to do at a young age was something that God would use me to do as an adult. I don't remember ever uttering the words, "*I want to be a preacher when I grow up.*"

Although I do not recall uttering those words as a child, God is the One who created me and decided how He wants to use me for His purpose, and to be honest, it is of great pleasure to be used for His purpose. It is a joy to serve God and His people through my gifts and talents. Say these words: *"I have great joy in what God has called me to do!"* Your assignments and purposes may not always have good days and may even bring some heartaches at times, but the joy of the Lord will sustain you. Your pursuit of what God has called you to do does not go away because of the bad times. There are times that I wanted to quit but could not because it is who I am and what I am called to do, and it brings me great joy.

Before we continue, let's discuss the similarities and differences regarding our gifts and talents. Both are given from God and used to serve or help others; however, a gift is a supernatural, spiritual ability given by God to believers, and a talent is a natural ability that can be passed down from your parents, or a skill that can be learned. One is natural, and the other is spiritual. I challenge you to study more on the difference between the two.

Read the following Scripture passages on spiritual gifts:

"Because of the privilege and authority God has given me, I give each of you this warning: Don't think you are better than you really are. Be honest in your evaluation of yourselves, measuring yourselves by the faith God has given us. Just as our bodies have many parts and each part has a special function, so it is with Christ's body. We are many parts of one body, and we all belong to each other.

In his grace, God has given us different gifts for doing certain things well. So if God has given you the ability to prophesy, speak out with as much faith as God has given you. If your gift is serving others, serve them well. If you are a teacher, teach well. If your gift is to encourage others, be encouraging. If it is giving, give generously. If God has given you leadership ability, take the responsibility seriously. And if you have a gift for showing kindness to others, do it gladly." Romans 12: 3-8 (NLT)

"To one person the Spirit gives the ability to give wise advice; to another the same Spirit gives a message of special knowledge. The same Spirit gives great faith to another, and to someone else the one Spirit gives the gift of healing. He gives one person the power to perform miracles, and another the ability to prophesy. He gives someone else the ability to discern whether a message is from the Spirit of God or from another spirit. Still another person is given the ability to speak in unknown languages] while another is given the ability to interpret what is being said. It is the one and only Spirit who distributes all these gifts. He alone decides which gift each person should have." 1 Corinthians 12: 8-11 (NLT)

"And the same one who descended is the one who ascended higher than all the heavens, so that he might fill the entire universe with himself. Now, these are the gifts Christ gave to the church: the apostles, the prophets, the evangelists, and the pastors, and teachers. Their responsibility is to equip God's people to do his work and build up the church, the body of Christ." Ephesians 4: 10-12 (NLT)

Make a list of your gifts and talents.

Talents	Gifts

"Good" idea...or "God" idea?

Advice to the creative: distractions can be "good" ideas but they are not always "God" ideas. Is it taking away from your foundation? In the previous chapter, I asked you to write down everything that you are doing or involved in. What part of it lines up with your assignment and purpose (your foundation)? List anything that you are doing in your life that is a distraction.

_____
_____
_____
_____

What are some tests that you find yourself repeating over and over again? Write those areas below and in the next column, write what you need to do differently in order to pass the test of life?

Test	Changes to Make

Begin to Build

Remember, Jesus Christ should be the foundation and included in anything that He has called us to do. Mastering a life of pursuit of Jesus Christ is always the first step to any assignment. Without a foundation built on Jesus Christ, you will guarantee yourself a breakdown when tests, trials, and tribulations come. As I stated before, *they will come*, but when you have Jesus Christ as your foundation, you will be sustained by the *peace, love, comfort, and strength* of God when those trials do come. Look at the diagram below. Write down a purpose or assignment that you believe God is calling you to as you pursue Him. In the next phase, write down the things that you need to do in order (no matter how small they seem), and continue until you see the manifestation of that purpose or assignment in your life. DO NOT move on to the next phase until you have completed everything in the first phase. You will come back to revisit this chapter.

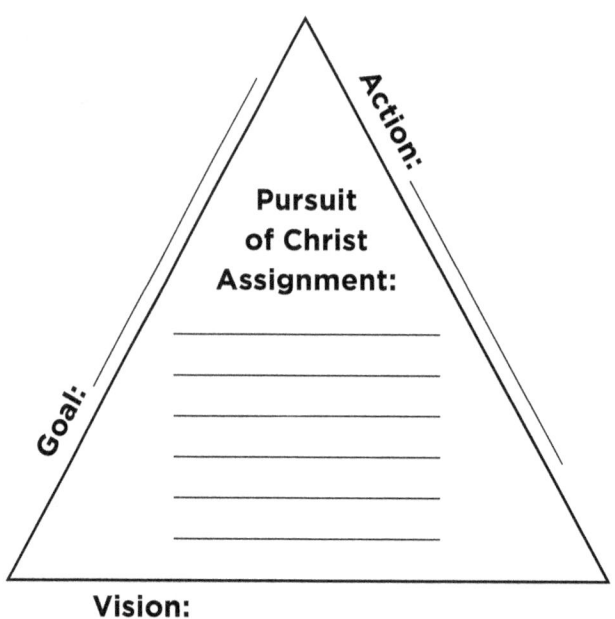

I want to provide you with an example. Writing a book was an **assignment** that God called me to. A completed book would have been the **vision**. My **goal** was to write an outline of the chapters: what would they include, etc. My **action** was to buy a laptop because I didn't have one at the time. Everyone's diagram will look different. As you seek direction from the Holy Spirit and wise counsel, He will provide you with the steps that need to take place in each phase.

Chapter 10

INVESTING IN YOURSELF

Growing in our assignments

In **Chapter 8**, you wrote down your talents, gifts, and passions. Do you know that there is always more to learn from our gifts and talents? We all still have room to grow; no one has "arrived," so to speak. We should be going from "faith-to-faith" and "glory-to-glory." We are to be constantly growing in who we are as women of God and constantly growing in our God-given assignments. Each year, you should be able to look back and see where you have improved and grown. Take the time right now to write down the areas in your life where you have grown. Are there areas where you have not grown?

Areas of Growth	Non-growth

Did you write anything in the second column? If so, those should be areas where you have a desire to grow. Reflect on your gifts and talents, and think about the areas that you would like to grow or improve on. For example, as an intercessor, I am always looking for ways to expand my prayer life. I do this by reading books on intercession and listening to other seasoned intercessors.

Begin to search out ways to invest in yourself, and write them down. You have already begun to invest in yourself because you decided to purchase this workbook and go through the journey of *TransHERmation*. Now it's time for you to expand. Invest in areas where individuals are seasoned in the areas that you are seeking growth. Invest in a mentor, a coach, Christian books, webinars, conferences, or training.

No investment...no return

You may be saying, "Why do I need to invest in myself?" *Because you are worth it!* When you give yourself value, it is easy to justify the investment in yourself. Without an investment, there is no return. There is something that you need; there is some knowledge to learn in order for you to excel. There is no way around investing in yourself as you walk out this walk of TransHERmation. If you are not willing to give, do not expect to receive. The knowledge that you invest in yourself through books, webinars, conferences, and/or trainings brings forth a harvest in your life. You are a seed that you need to nurture by investing in you! God has placed vessels (people of God) before you that you can glean from; and one day, others will glean and invest in you as you walk out your purpose(s) and assignments. Take this time to read **page 189 – "***Investing in you***"** in my book *TransHERmation*.

Read *I Kings 17:7-16*: Elijah and the poor widow. After you read this passage, write down some insights that you received.

"But after a while the brook dried up, for there was no rainfall anywhere in the land.

Then the Lord said to Elijah, 'Go and live in the village of Zarephath, near the city of Sidon. I have instructed a widow there to feed you.'

So he went to Zarephath. As he arrived at the gates of the village, he saw a widow gathering sticks, and he asked her, 'Would you please bring me a little water in a cup?' As she was going to get it, he called to her, 'Bring me a bite of bread, too.'

But she said, 'I swear by the Lord your God that I don't have a single piece of bread in the house. And I have only a handful of flour left in the jar and a little cooking oil in the bottom of the jug. I was just gathering a few sticks to cook this last meal, and then my son and I will die.'

But Elijah said to her, 'Don't be afraid! Go ahead and do just what you've said, but make a little bread for me first. Then use what's left to prepare a meal for yourself and your son. For this is what the Lord, the God of Israel, says: There will always be flour and olive oil left in your containers until the time when the Lord sends rain and the crops grow again!'

So she did as Elijah said, and she and Elijah and her family continued to eat for many days. There was always enough flour and olive oil left in the containers, just as the Lord had promised through Elijah." (NLT)

_____
_____
_____
_____
_____
_____

Because she trusted and believed God, she wasn't poor anymore. Her investment reaped a reward.

Are you waiting on a perfect opportunity or the right time to invest? Are you waiting on it to rain in your life before you invest? The poor widow did not wait until it rained before she invested. She obeyed the voice of the Lord through Elijah.

Read **Ecclesiastes 11:1-6 VS 4: Message Translation: "If you wait until the wind and the weather are just right, you will never plant anything and never harvest anything."**

Planting a seed in someone else is an investment in your life that will be a wealth of knowledge to you and will be a lasting step to breaking the poverty mentality.

Write down how you are going to invest in each area. Give yourself a timeline and *stick to it*. Side note: Everything does not have to cost a lot of money and some things will not require money, but all will require *commitment*, *faithfulness*, and *time*.

Spiritual	Financial	Health & Wellness	Gift	Talent

Chapter 11

CROWNED LADY: WEARING YOUR PRIESTLY GARMENTS

Dress for success!

I *see* you, Shining Woman of God! I *know* you are believing and trusting in who God has called you to be. I *know* you have begun the process of walking out your purpose and assignment on the Earth. I *know* the Holy Spirit has imparted in you to move forward! If by chance you are still stuck in a place of stagnation, I challenge you to start back with **Chapter 1** and decide in your heart that you are ready to go on a journey of TransHERmation. The Lord Jesus Christ is drawing you closer to Himself...because if He wasn't, you wouldn't have this workbook in your hand! I am a Woman of Faith...and I *know* God doesn't make mistakes. I am excited about how far you have come through this journey. I know sometimes it has been rough, especially dealing with matters of the heart. It is a good thing to come to the light because the light exposes the dark (what is not of God): those evil, undesirable areas. Jesus is the light, and He wants to present you as a jewel for His Glory. Your very purpose on the Earth is actually God's purpose being manifested through you. You are the vessel. **Job 42:2: "I know that you can do everything, and that no purpose of yours can be withheld from you."** Woman of God, He is smiling on you because you have surrendered your will for His.

Now that you know who you are in Jesus Christ and now that you have been changed inwardly – it's time for the change to manifest outwardly.

Excerpt from page 187: *A woman of TransHERmation: "Do you not know that God cares about every aspect of your life, both spiritually and physically? We started this workbook dealing with our inner man first because it makes no sense to adorn yourself outwardly without inner change."* **"What profits a man if he gains the whole world yet forfeit their soul." Mark 8:36 (NLT)**

We are women of royalty, and it's time for you to allow your Heavenly Father to adorn you outwardly. I know you may be thinking, "Doesn't God look at the heart and not the outer appearance?" You are absolutely correct. However, in the context that God spoke this Word, He was looking to appoint a king over the people after King Saul was rejected by God. Jesse had seven sons that were to be presented before the prophet Samuel. Each son was rejected except for David, who was the youngest son, and a sheepherder. God told Samuel in *I Samuel 16:7:* **"Don't judge by his appearance or height, for I have rejected him. The Lord doesn't see things the way you see them. People judge by outward appearance, but the Lord looks at the heart."**

Take the time to read *I Samuel 16:1-13*:

"Now the Lord said to Samuel, 'You have mourned long enough for Saul. I have rejected him as king of Israel, so fill your flask with olive oil and go to Bethlehem. Find a man named Jesse who lives there, for I have selected one of his sons to be my king.'

But Samuel asked, 'How can I do that? If Saul hears about it, he will kill me.'

'Take a heifer with you,' the Lord replied, 'and say that you have come to make a sacrifice to the Lord. Invite Jesse to the sacrifice, and I will show you which of his sons to anoint for me.'

So Samuel did as the Lord instructed. When he arrived at Bethlehem, the elders of the town came trembling to meet him. 'What's wrong?' they asked. 'Do you come in peace?'

'Yes,' Samuel replied. 'I have come to sacrifice to the Lord. Purify yourselves and come with me to the sacrifice.' Then Samuel performed the purification rite for Jesse and his sons and invited them to the sacrifice, too.

When they arrived, Samuel took one look at Eliab and thought, 'Surely this is the Lord's anointed!'

But the Lord said to Samuel, 'Don't judge by his appearance or height, for I have rejected him. The Lord doesn't see things the way you see them. People judge by outward appearance, but the Lord looks at the heart.'

Then Jesse told his son Abinadab to step forward and walk in front of Samuel. But Samuel said, 'This is not the one the Lord has chosen." Next Jesse summoned Shimea, but Samuel said, 'Neither is this the one the Lord has chosen.' In the same way all seven of Jesse's sons were presented to Samuel. But Samuel said to Jesse, 'The Lord has not chosen any of these.' Then Samuel asked, 'Are these all the sons you have?'

'There is still the youngest,' Jesse replied. 'But he's out in the fields watching the sheep and goats.'

'Send for him at once,' Samuel said. 'We will not sit down to eat until he arrives.'

So Jesse sent for him. He was dark and handsome, with beautiful eyes.

And the Lord said, 'This is the one; anoint him.' So as David stood there among his brothers, Samuel took the flask of olive oil he had brought and anointed David with the oil. And the Spirit of the Lord came powerfully upon David from that day on. Then Samuel returned to Ramah." (NLT)

It's a heart thing

This passage tells you that God doesn't choose you based on your outward appearance, whether you are rich or poor, have a degree or not, live in good neighborhood or bad neighborhood, have attained a certain socio-economic status, the position you hold at your job or the level of experience that you have, etc. **He chooses you based on what He sees in your heart.**

It would seem more logical for God to choose a king that was older and more experienced in battle, war, and life in general, but it was David's heart that God looked upon. God anointed King David to fulfill the assignment of a king because he had the right heart. It was God that supernaturally gave David the ability to carry out the assignment because God could trust Him. King David's assignment was expanded.

Jeremiah 17:10: "But I, the Lord, search all hearts and examine secret motives. I give all people their due rewards, according to what their actions deserve." At this moment, you should start saying, "Thank you Jesus!" and shouting, "**Hallelujah!,**" because He chose you to walk out Kingdom purposes and assignments.

Write out *I Samuel 16:6-7*

_____
_____
_____
_____

Underline the word "appearance." Appearance in the context of the Scripture is referring to looks, shape, handsome – in our case beautiful.

Read *I Samuel 16:11-12* again, and write down everything that pertains to David (including his occupation and physical appearance.)

David: _____
_____
_____
_____

Eliab: _____
_____
_____
_____

From the descriptions of the brothers, they were both handsome in appearance. It may have seemed more "logical" to anoint the tall, oldest, handsomest brother, and not the youngest, shortest brother whose occupation was herding sheep. Remember, God said He does not choose based on physical appearance or stature. It appeared as if David was the weaker brother because of his outer appearance but in all actuality, he was the one with the greatest strength and courage.

Take the time to Read *I Samuel 17*. David was not afraid to confront Goliath, when the others were terrified. Eliab, David's oldest brother, was the one to speak against David after God had already chosen him and declared that he was a man after His own heart.

Read *I Samuel 17:28* and *Acts 13:22*, and write them below.

_____
_____
_____
_____

What are some characteristics of David's heart that you noticed after reading these passages? Write them below.

_____
_____
_____
_____

Remember: God chose David based on his heart and then changed his status as a king. Once your status changes, *everything* about you changes, even your outer appearance.

Take the time now to read *Jeremiah 52:31-33*, regarding a king by the name of Jehoiachin.

"In the thirty-seventh year of the exile of King Jehoiachin of Judah, Evil-Merodach ascended to the Babylonian throne. He was kind to Jehoiachin and released him from prison on March 31 of that year. He spoke kindly to Jehoiachin and gave him a higher place than all the other exiled kings in Babylon. He supplied Jehoiachin with new clothes to replace his prison garb and allowed him to dine in the king's presence for the rest of his life." (NLT)

Write **Jeremiah 52:33** below. What did you notice about this verse?

_____
_____
_____
_____

Woman of God, your status has changed. Now you will adorn yourself as a princess and a queen. Your assignment and purpose, no matter what it is, is going to bring you before people, and those people may not necessarily be believers or people that can see your heart as God sees it. Man *does* look at the outer appearance; therefore, you must present yourself accordingly.

Take this time to read **Chapter 22, page 186:** *"Excellence of Appearance."* How does this section speak to you?

_____
_____
_____
_____
_____
_____
_____

A new woman!

What are some lies that you have accepted from the enemy as truths? Begin to reject those lies. The lie that you accept is what will manifest. Whatever lies the enemy has spoken in your mind or may have spoken through others, do not accept them. Hold up your hand and say, "I don't receive it, in Jesus Name!" You have to know your triggers, so that you can know your enemy and reject him!

Are there areas where you have neglected yourself in the past, because you didn't feel worthy or valued? You are no longer that woman. Are there areas that you have neglected in your appearance? For example, your hair, nails, shoes, or an outfit? When was the last time you got your hair done, bought a new outfit or a pair of shoes, went to get a pedicure or a massage, or treated yourself to a facial? Don't worry about going to buy something expensive. As you just read on page 186, we women can make any outfit look like a million bucks.

Woman of God, it's your time!

Chapter 12

WORDS OF WISDOM

I want to congratulate you on completing this workbook! I know you are being transformed and are ready to walk out everything that God has for you. God is developing you in the secret places, and will reveal you openly as you humble yourself before Him and submit to the process of being changed in His image. I know it isn't always easy, but as I said, it is all worth it. It is all worth pleasing our Heavenly Father!

When you become transformed, others will look at you and say W.O.W! Surely you are a **W**oman **o**f **W**isdom! TransHERmation always starts with the heart. ***"Whatsoever a man thinketh in his heart, so is he." Proverbs 23:7 (KJV)***

Remaining firmly grounded in the Word

Once you hear and receive the message of the good news and gospel of Jesus Christ and believe the Word—that Jesus is the Son of God that shed His blood, died for your sins, and rose on the third day and is still living today, the Holy Spirit comes to live on the inside of you. The Holy Spirit is on the inside of you as your Helper, and your Helper is there to comfort, strengthen, and reveal all truth to you. The truth comes from the Word of God and what God has spoken over your life. The Word of God holds all truth, and your spirit will bear witness to the truth of the Word of God. There are truths in the Word of God that declares that you are more than a conqueror; victorious through Christ Jesus; the apple of His eye; a friend of God to those that obey Him; and the list goes on and on.

Get in the Word of God to see what He says about you. Once you hear what the Word of God says concerning you, then confess it with your mouth, and ask God to fill your heart with the very words that you have confessed. Your spirit should only bear witness to the truth, and your spirit should reject a lie. When someone says that you will never amount to anything, you are worthless, you are ugly, you will always be broke, you will never succeed…whatever those words are…you should begin to reject those words and declare the opposite and pray for God to fill your heart with what He has spoken. It is only when you reject negativity and ill-spoken words, come under agreement with God's Word, confess it, and receive His Word in your heart that you will begin to see the manifestation. **"Faith is the substance of things hoped for, and the evidence of things not seen." Hebrews 11:1 (NLT)** God is the Author and Finisher of our faith. Faith begins with faith in Him. You cannot "muster up" faith, because faith begins and ends with our trust and belief in Jesus Christ. With faith comes instructions. Whatever and whomever God is telling you to let go of, make sure you do it immediately. Make sure you are obeying the instructions of God for your life. You may not see immediate manifestations but trust God, you will see manifestations as you obey Him! Woman of God, hear the Word of the Lord concerning your life. You were created to serve Him by walking out your God-given purpose on this Earth. Are there limitations currently operating in your life? Declare the Word of the Lord and see yourself without those limitations, and watch God fulfill His divine will over your life.

"So faith comes from hearing, that is, hearing the Good News about Christ." Romans 10:17 (NLT) Hear the Good News and respond to what you hear! May your faith be activated to be all that God has called you to be! In Jesus' Name, Amen!

This workbook is designed for you to continue to go back to the chapters for reflection and maintenance during any stage of your life. TransHERmation is a lifetime journey, and we should always be growing. Feel free to go back through this workbook six months from now, a year from now, or whenever you need to be reminded of His love for you. I encourage you to repeat this workbook at least three times in a row so that what you have learned will take root. You will also see areas of growth and areas that still need extra attention. The journey of TransHERmation takes discipline. It will be well worth it in the end.

Bonus Chapter

FASTING

Out with the old, in with the new

Fasting is to deny yourself food for a period of time. Fasting is denying your flesh and submitting your will to the will of God. It is humbling yourself before God and surrendering your total will to His direction. Fasting is a time of emptying out the old to make room for the new. It is a time to repent from sin, obtain direction and instruction, and obtain favor, protection, and comfort during times of loss. This is a time to be broken before God, and a time to strengthen your inner man with the spirit of might (God's power). As you begin to choose a fast, walking into being transformed in the image of God and walking out your purpose, I encourage you to start with a fast of repentance. Repentance is a time for you to make a decision that you are removing yourself from old habits—from your old ways and your sinful nature. It is a time to declare that you are a new creature in Jesus Christ and walking as a new Woman of God that is led by God and not your emotions, fleshly, and sinful nature.

Fasting denies your flesh for a length of time to gain a greater strength spiritually; your focus is clearer on a fast. You will receive insights and revelations from God as you set this time aside to pray, worship, meditate, and read your Bible! If you remove food from yourself for a specific amount of time but do not take the time to pray and read the Word, you are simply on a diet. No sacrifice = no deposit! I highly encourage you to fast and pray for the heart and mind of God and to be transformed into everything He has called you to be. If this is your first time fasting, remember that everyone has to start somewhere. Do what you can. Try denying yourself sweets, snacks, or meat for four hours...do something and watch God honor your sincere sacrifice! Be patient and wait on Him to bring forth and birth out everything He has for you. Patience is one of the fruits of the Spirit. Check out one of my Facebook posts on patience…I had to bring this forward, Woman of God, before we officially close!

There are times when people say, "Be careful what you pray for…don't pray for patience because God just might give it to you!" Patience or longsuffering is a fruit of the spirit and produced by the Holy Spirit, and as believers, we *shouldn't avoid* praying for patience/longsuffering. Patience enables us to not be easily provoked, easily offended, quick-tempered, or easily angered. Patience allows us to be slow to anger. We need patience to endure hardships, persecutions, trials, and tribulations because some of our hardships are long lasting. Oftentimes, the process can seem long lasting and without patience, and we may give up easily, lose our faith, or potentially react in a manner that is contrary to the fruit of the spirit. Change your outlook on patience…because we *cannot desire the fruit of the spirit and leave out patience*. May your outlook change on praying for patience, as mine has. #PrayforPatience

The benefits of fasting

- Brings us **closer to God** and His presence: ***Matthew 9:14-17***.
- The **anointing increases** in your life.
- You will receive **deeper revelations** from God.
- You will experience **many breakthroughs**.
- The **authority** of God, power of God, and faith of God **comes alive**.
- Your spirit man **becomes stronger**.
- **Breaks** yokes and heavy burdens: ***Isaiah 58***.
- Brings **freedom** from demonic spirits: ***Matthew 17:21***.
- **Humility** and a **closer walk** with God.
- Open **rewards**: ***Matthew 6:17-18***.
- **Purging** and **cleansing** from sin.

Fasting is NOT

- Fasting is **not** a way to manipulate God into doing what "you" desire; He is not a genie or magician. We do not fast to move God towards *our* agenda; but instead, to find out what *His* agenda is. Praying your will on a person or situation is also known as "soulish prayers."

- Fasting is **not** to be done out of pride; be sincere, humble, and open to receive instruction and correction from God.
- Fasting is **not** hypocritical or religious as the Pharisees fasted: The Pharisees fasted to be seen and out of ritual rather than having a true sincere relationship with God. The Pharisees did not see their need to have a relationship with God, because according to them, they were fine because they were observing the law, rituals, and traditions of the Torah. The Pharisees felt they had a relationship with Him because they knew the Scriptures (see **Matthew 6:16-18**.)

Remember! Fasting without prayer and reading the Bible is just a diet!

Looking at Isaiah 58

Read **Isaiah 58** and in the space below, write down what fasting is not, and what godly fasting looks like. If there is anything in this chapter that you do not understand, begin to pray and ask the Holy Spirit to give you revelation.

Godly fasting is *Not*...	Godly fasting *is*...

Biblical Fasting

- Corporate prayer: ***I Samuel 7:5-6.***
- Humbling yourself: ***I Kings 21:27-29.***
- Healing and mercy: ***2 Samuel 12:13-15.***
- Protection and escape from the enemy; the king was ordained to put Daniel in the lion's den: ***Daniel 6:13-18.***
- Repentance: ***I Samuel 7:6, Nehemiah 9:1, Jerimiah 36:6-10***.

- Healing: ***Isaiah 58:8; Acts 9:9, 17-19.***
- Seeking God's direction in a given situation: ***Judges 20:26-28, 2 Chronicles 20:3-4.***
- Intercession for the people of God: ***Deuteronomy 9:8-9, 12-20, 23-27, Joel 2:12-13, Joel 2:17-18, Daniel 9:3-4.***
- Asking the Lord for safety and protection: ***Ezra 8:21-23.***
- Petitioning God to withhold His hand of judgment: ***Deuteronomy 9:18.***
- Deliverance from demonic spirits; some of these come out only by fasting and prayer: ***Matthew 17:21, Mark 9:29.***
- God's favor and protection: ***Esther 4:16.***
- When choosing and ordaining leaders in the church: ***Acts 14:23, Acts 13:2-3.***
- Mercy: ***Jonah 3:6-10.***
- Mourning the loss of a loved one: ***2 Samuel 1:12, I Samuel 31:13, 2 Samuel 3:35.***
- Grieving over the injustice of an individual or individuals: ***Isaiah 58:6.***

Biblical Fasting and Duration

- **Jesus:** forty days and forty nights; no food or drink; ***Matthew 4:2, Mark 1:13, Luke 4:2.***
- **Daniel:** twenty-one days; ***Daniel 10:3-13***.
- **Esther:** three days and three nights; no food or drink; ***Esther 4:16***.
- **King David:** seven days; ***II Samuel 12:16-23.***
- **Moses:** forty days; ***Exodus 24:18; 34:28.***
- **The king in the Book of Daniel:** one night; ***Daniel 6:18.***
- **The Israelites:** one day; ***Judges 20:26.***

Partial Fast: Abstain from *some* food and drink for a period of time.

Absolute Fast: Abstain from *all* food and drink for a period of time.

Daniel Fast: Abstain from *certain* foods for 21 days. This type of fast usually consists of fruits, vegetables, and grains.

40-Day Fast should be led by the Holy Spirit and should be done under a doctor's care, especially if you have health concerns.

Bonus Fasting Assignment

Purpose: To humble yourself and draw closer to God by asking Him to search your heart and reveal the things that need to be purged, seek His mercy in those areas, and pray for loved ones, friends, and enemies that need God's mercy. Are there specific areas in your life that you need the hand of God to touch? This could be healing, finances, promotion, protection of a loved one, a negative report to be turned positive…

7 Day Fast: fruits, vegetables, whole grains, (brown rice, oatmeal, whole grain bread), nuts, and beans only. No dairy of any kind including cheese, milk, eggs, or yogurt.

If you are under a doctor's care or have health restrictions, limit your fasting to what you can do. Please continue with those restrictions under your doctor's care.

Prayer Nugget

There are eight prayer watches. I encourage you to study them, but for the purpose of this exercise, we are going to focus on the fourth watch, which takes place between 3:00 a.m. – 6:00 a.m.

Fourth Watch (The Morning Watch from 3:00 A.M. to 6:00 A.M.)

This fourth watch is important because this is the last watch of the night. This is the time that satanic agents who have been out and about performing their activities are returning to their bases. It was during this watch that the Israelites were delivered from slavery in Egypt **(Exodus 12 and 14).** It was also the watch when Jesus walked on the water to help the disciples who were caught in the storm **(Matthew 14:25-33)**. This is the time to establish the course of your day by speaking God's Word and breaking everything that would attempt to hinder His will for your life to manifest on third day. **(Psalm 19:2)**.

Conclusion

I am so proud of you for taking a leap of faith by completing not only this workbook, but this fast. I am believing God and praying *with* and *for* you that every desire of your heart that God has planted in you will come to pass with no delay. I believe that you are breaking free with confidence and boldness to become your unique self. My prayer is that you will continue to discover more of you and go from faith to faith and glory to glory!

Appendix A

Proverbs

Read a chapter in the Book of Proverbs daily and write down the key points regarding wisdom and other wise counsel that Solomon provides in each chapter.

Chapter	Key Verse	Wisdom/Counsel
1		
2		
3		
4		
5		
6		
7		
8		
9		
10		
11		
12		
13		
14		
15		
16		
17		
18		

19		
20		
21		
22		
23		
24		
25		
26		
27		
28		
29		
30		
31		

Moments of Reflection

Date	Lesson/Reflection

Evaluate Your Relationships

Name	Relationship	Benefit

Resources

Scriptures to help you combat the lies of the enemy

Phil. 4:13: "I can do all things through Christ who strengthens me." (NLT)

Romans 8:31: "What, then, shall we say in response to these things? If God is for us, who can be against us?" (NLT)

Ephesians 2:10 "For we are God's masterpiece. He has created us anew in Christ Jesus, so we can do the good things he planned for us long ago." (NLT)

Psalm 139:14: "Thank you for making me so wonderfully complex! Your workmanship is marvelous-how well I know it." (NLT)

Deuteronomy 3:16: "So be strong and courageous! Do not be afraid and do not panic before them. For the Lord your God will personally go ahead of you. He will neither fail you nor abandon you." (NLT).

About the Author

Minister Lakeea Kelly is a native of Battle Creek, MI, and a member of New Harvest Christian Center, under Pastors Ivan and Tina Lee. She serves on the Ministerial Team, ministering at the local jail and women's shelter. Minister Lakeea accepted Jesus Christ into her life at the age of nine, again at twelve, and decided to live sold out for Jesus at the age of twenty-nine. She is married to Elder Dwayne Kelly, and they have four children and four grandchildren. In 2006, Minister Lakeea obtained a bachelor's degree in Family Life Education from Spring Arbor University and has studied Counseling Psychology at Western Michigan University. She is currently pursuing her Master's Degree in Psychology with an Emphasis on Life Coaching at Grand Canyon University.

Minister Lakeea is an author, entrepreneur, and certified coach. She loves to empower, impart and build people up to be all that God has called them to be. Additionally, Minister Lakeea carries a mantle of intercession, with a passion for the gospel of Jesus Christ, and a desire to see souls saved, healed, and delivered. She enjoys being a mentor and coach to women by empowering them through encouragement, godly counsel, the Word of God, and prayer. Minister Lakeea's passion for the lives of others is consistently demonstrated in her family, church, and community.

Contact the Author

LakeeaKelly@gmail.com
www.transhermation.com
Facebook: https://www.facebook.com/Transhermation/

www.ingramcontent.com/pod-product-compliance
Lightning Source LLC
Chambersburg PA
CBHW051213290426
44109CB00021B/2441